Focus Like a Laser Beam

10 Ways to Do What Matters Most

Lisa Haneberg

Foreword by Keith Ferrazzi

JOSSEY-BASS
A Wiley Imprint
www.josseybass.com

Published by Jossey-Bass
A Wiley Imprint
989 Market Street, San Francisco, CA 94103-1741   www.josseybass.com

Jossey-Bass books and products are available through most bookstores. To contact Jossey-Bass directly call our Customer Care Department within the U.S. at 800-956-7739, outside the U.S. at 317-572-3986, or fax 317-572-4002.

Jossey-Bass also publishes its books in a variety of electronic formats. Some content that appears in print may not be available in electronic books.

Library of Congress Cataloging-in-Publication Data

Haneberg, Lisa.
   Focus like a laser beam : 10 ways to do what matters most / Lisa Haneberg ; foreword by Keith Ferrazzi.
       p. cm.
   Includes bibliographical references and index.
   ISBN-13: 978-0-7879-8481-6 (cloth)
   ISBN-10: 0-7879-8481-7 (cloth)
   1. Executive ability. 2. Leadership. 3. Management. 4. Organizational effectiveness. I. Title.
   HD38.2.H363 2006
   658.4'09—dc22

                                                              2006010545

Printed in the United States of America
FIRST EDITION
HB Printing   10 9 8 7 6 5 4 3 2 1

Contents

Foreword

In my book *Never Eat Alone*, I shared numerous stories that make the case for building real relationships to grow our revenue, to accelerate our careers, and even to put more joy into time spent with our families and closest friends. And when *Never Eat Alone* caused my path to cross with Lisa Haneberg's, I was thrilled to hear that she was championing the same point: that the strength of our relationships has a significant impact on our ability to focus our organizations on what's most important.

Many leaders underestimate the power of an energized and connected workplace. Fortunately, you won't be one of them after reading this book. As Lisa eloquently illustrates in *Focus Like a Laser Beam*, when our people are jazzed about their work and in tune with each other, they can make truly amazing things happen. I have experienced this firsthand, through all the challenges and joys of running Ferrazzi Greenlight, my consulting and professional development firm. Sure, we benefit from having talented people, but we gain even more from the way those talented people are energized by and connected to their work and each other. How do we achieve such focus? Many candid conversations.

Lisa has said, "Leadership is a social act. It occurs in conversations. It makes sense, then, that leaders need to be master conversationalists, because this is the currency by which they produce results." That's a powerful thought. Talk, dialogue, or conversation, whatever you want to call it, is how we as leaders make things happen. Mathematicians may need to learn equations and use complex computer programs. Astronomers had better know how to work a telescope. But for leaders, conversation is the primary tool we use to get things done. I love the ideas that Lisa shares in this book for improving dialogue in the workplace.

Focus Like a Laser Beam is not your typical book on productivity. When you recognize that, as we say at Ferrazzi Greenlight, "Business is human," you know that no amount of organizational tips, to-do list tactics, or multitasking techniques will give you the results you want. To accomplish the feats to which we aspire today, we need much more. We need to implement the ten practices Lisa offers us here.

March 2006   Keith Ferrazzi
                                     CEO, Ferrazzi Greenlight
                                     Author of *Never Eat Alone:*
                                     And Other Secrets to Success,
                                     One Relationship at a Time

INTRODUCTION

This book is about focus, jacked up on steroids and at a new level that few have experienced and of which only some have dreamed. You have seen laser focus in action. How is it that a black belt in karate can put a hand through hard wooden boards? How does a team of Olympic athletes come together to create a world-class upset and break all known records for performance? How does a professional golfer apply the most delicate and precise touch to sink a long putt while surrounded by thousands of staring eyes? How does a product development team imbue every move with creativity and fuse their vision to create innovative treasures ahead of the competition? How does an organization become beloved by customers, stockholders, and employees at the same time? The ability to focus helps separate the good from the great in all professions and disciplines. To achieve laser focus, leaders transcend conventional methods and adjust their beliefs about productivity and performance.

Conventional thinking and even tried-and-true practices are not enough. The everyday barrage of tough and demanding business problems consumes leaders; it drenches them with distractions, stress, and the morphing needs and ills that require even the best to move faster than hummingbirds. But humans are not hummingbirds, and they can't work around the clock to try to keep up. Even if they could, it would be of no use. To conquer the speed of business, like the speed of light, we need new vehicles that attack the problem from a different perspective.

If you looked up the meaning of focus, you would find several definitions. Focus means attention on the right things. Focusing means concentrating attention or energy on something. To focus is to achieve maximum clarity or a distinct vision. When you focus you concentrate on something or a central point. These definitions are all fine, but they are vague and do not offer much in the way of suggestions for action. They do not adequately describe the things that are unique about sharp focus in a business setting. The secrets to achieving focus must lie elsewhere.

Managers meandering through their workday don't fall in and out of focus without knowing that it has happened. One cannot accidentally focus. Focusing involves intention and choice. Focus and attention are not the same, not by a long shot. You give many topics your attention, but focus on few. General attention is shallow and rests on the surface. Focus is deep and selective. Attention can be passive, but focus is active.

Many leaders know that the usual definitions, tips, and techniques are woefully inadequate in today's ever-changing global business climate. Even companies with previously stable products, services, and business challenges have to rethink the ways in which they go to market and compete. Leaders are confused. They want to be optimistic and energetic about the future, but they spend much of their time mourning the loss of their ability to manage it all and remain sane. When it comes to the ways in which leaders work, years of past success can become a barrier to future achievement. To realize quantum leaps in results, a leader needs to focus like a laser beam.

Laser beams are beautiful. Each bit of energy is jazzed to the max and moves in harmony. Their complicated inner soul creates an outer appearance that is elegantly simple and straightforward: literally straight forward. Forward an inch wide and mile long. Strong, intense, and determined to reach the target with precision. One mind, one purpose, one direction. And while the laser is not the brightest light in any one moment, it goes farther, farther, miles farther and faster on track. Crazed, long, pure, and smooth.

Lasers are among the best and most practical applications of quantum mechanics. They are special and their properties hold secrets for today's busy leaders. This book offers a new way to focus that gets its inspiration from characteristics of laser beams as described by professor Mark Csele in *Fundamentals of Light Sources and Lasers* (2004). Each part of this book zeros in on one goal:

Part One ("Excite and Energize") offers leaders ways to improve energy and engagement in the workplace. When employees are energized, they are more interested and better able to focus on what's most important. *Energy is a powerful catalyst for creating focus.*

Part Two ("Tune Your Dialogue") will help leaders change what people talk about at work. Reality is constructed in conversation; if you want to change the topics, tasks, or projects on which people focus, you need to change how they converse. *Work dialogue is the vehicle for focus.*

Part Three ("Zoom In") details leadership practices that will help you focus on what's most important and deal with distractions and diversions. *To focus, leaders must zoom in close.*

The three goals of laser beam focus are simple and straightforward, but they also pack a punch. To achieve focus, you will want to fuel up your organization so it can move with great velocity (energy and excitement) and create a compelling future that takes center stage in work conversations (tuned dialogue). To focus your resources and do things well, you and your team should determine how to best use your precious time (zooming in).

Many techniques support these three goals. This book offers ten that will produce great results with minimal effort. Each chapter explains and highlights one practice. Here are the ways I propose to help you do what matters most:

- *Know and feel the power of laser focus:* Chapter One helps you distinguish and assess your focus. Examples illustrate how laser focus looks and feels.
- *Get intimate with your employees:* Connected employees care more about their work, are more focused, and produce better

results. Chapter Two makes the case for intimacy at work and offers suggestions for pumping up energy through connection.

- *Have fun and be fun:* Fun is fun! You can be laser-focused on the business and a lot of fun to work with. Chapter Three offers several techniques that leaders can use to create a work environment that is fun, focused, and productive.

- *Relax to energize:* Stress and mental fatigue rob leaders of their ability to focus and succeed. Chapter Four offers several ways to enhance your mental capabilities that you can incorporate into your busy day.

- *Turn meetings into focus sessions:* Leaders often put meetings on the top of the list of time wasters. Intuitively they know that meeting about a project or work topic should improve progress and understanding. Chapter Five explains how you can turn everyday meetings into powerful tools of focus and results.

- *Invite a challenge:* Laser focus is highly active and thrives on new ideas and healthy curiosity. Chapter Six establishes the value of a challenge and shares several ways leaders can request and receive constructive challenges.

- *Huddle:* How do the best organizations stay in touch and focused on a daily and hourly basis? Chapter Seven offers the virtues of huddling and shares specific examples for how to make huddles a key part of your managerial practice.

- *Stop multitasking:* Laser-focused leaders know that multitasking saps their organization of focus, energy, and productivity. Chapter Eight explains why multitasking is ineffective and what to do instead.

- *Do one great thing:* Many leaders leave the office frustrated that they did not accomplish more during the day. So many distractions get in the way of best intentions. Chapter Nine helps leaders accomplish at least one great thing every day.

- *Let go:* As goals, projects, and tasks become obsolete, leaders need to let go and use their energy and resources to focus on what now matters most. Chapter Ten makes the case for letting go of the old and suggests ways to know when it is time to adopt and commit to a new focus.

These ten practices can help you do what matters most without requiring you to take on a new management system. Each chapter offers ways to improve focus that fit nicely into any leadership practice. *Focus Like a Laser Beam* should appeal to many reading styles. It offers the following features:

- *In a Nutshell:* Each chapter begins with a quick summary of the theory and techniques presented. This section will appeal to those readers who prefer scanning for ideas.
- *Key Point:* The text calls out major concepts to make them easier to review and recall.
- *In the Real World:* The final section of each chapter offers examples of how to put techniques into action.

Reflect on some accomplishments that at first seemed impossible, improbable, and out of reach. Perhaps it was a contingency response or a project about which everyone was unusually enthusiastic. You likely shifted into a mode in which you were engaged, zoomed in, and in constant conversation. Diversions stuck out like a double-breasted suit at a Jimmy Buffet concert. A little magic, a splash of luck, and a lot of effort allowed you and your team to cross the victory line. Laser focus taps into the actions and thinking processes that will allow you to recreate this environment without putting your organization into contingency mode or tiring your team.

Laser beams are supercharged, efficient, and endlessly useful. *Focus Like a Laser Beam* draws on these and other properties of lasers to explore a powerful new productivity model. The techniques and practices are catalysts that complement your daily management and leadership actions. The laser beam model and practices enable you to clarify, crystallize, and energize your direction and effectiveness by catalyzing the three fundamental business resources—vitality, dialogue, and time. Most work environments are awash in a jumble of colors, conversations, and stimuli. Leaders who focus like a laser beam have figured out how to create success using energy, cohesion, and intentionality.

About the Title

I first heard the phrase "focus like a laser beam" while working for Black & Decker in the late 1980s. Joe Galli was vice president of marketing for the Power Tools Division, and was leading the product development and launch of the DeWalt line of power tools. The DeWalt product line was a big deal, a make-or-break moment for Black & Decker's market share in the increasingly popular do-it-yourself stores like Home Depot and Lowes. The new products needed to be innovative and comprehensive, beautiful tools designed to meet most every need on the construction site or in the home. To get it all done, Black & Decker needed to develop products faster and better than it ever had. Consumer needs and wants needed to be crystallized into excellent product designs. I can remember hearing Joe Galli say on many occasions, "We need to focus like a laser beam." He would pinch his thumb and forefinger together and stretch them out, simulating the straight and narrow shape of a laser. At product team meetings, at company briefings, and during general business conversation, he would repeat, "Focus like a laser beam."

I have never forgotten Galli's mantra and the effect it had on the DeWalt launch. Products were created in record time and to high standards. The DeWalt line was and has been a great success for Black & Decker. Whenever I feel overwhelmed because I have taken on too many projects at once, I remember to focus like a laser beam. Looking back on that time at Black & Decker, I can see that the DeWalt teams had laser focus. The environment was highly energized, great dialogue replaced the usual business banter, and distractions were quickly defenestrated.

My interest in focus grew after working on the DeWalt launch. At the same time, I developed an interest in lasers themselves and quantum physics (from a layperson's view). What I discovered is that characteristics of lasers can be applied to improve business focus. This brought new meaning to focusing like a laser beam! It is a thrill to share these techniques with you.

Part One

EXCITE AND ENERGIZE

This is the magic of the laser, the concept of
stimulated emission.

—Mark Csele

Lasers work by virtue of an amazing phenomenon known as *stimulated emission* of photons, which are packets of energy that behave as both waves and particles. Albert Einstein discovered stimulated emission in 1916, but the idea was forgotten for more than thirty years. To create a laser beam, a seed photon is sent down a tube filled with atoms that have been excited by pumping them with electricity or light. When the seed photon passes by an excited atom, the atom emits a photon that is the exact duplicate—a clone—of the first photon and transfers some of its energy in the process. Now there are two photons, which will pass by two more atoms to create two more identical photons. All are the same wavelength (color) and in phase. The atoms and photons don't collide; they simply need to pass near each other for stimulated emission to occur. Soon, countless photons are bouncing back and forth between the mirrors at each end of the laser. The light bounces back and forth between the mirrors until it has enough energy and alignment to escape an optical opening at one end.

Back in the workplace, the air is electric. It buzzes and bellows a common tune sung by many unique voices. What first resembles a chaotic New York subway station is organized and in control. It is the buzz that fools people. Leaders who know how to focus and ensure their teams' focus have mastered the art of imbuing the workplace with excitement and energy. Atoms in a laser are supercharged and stimulated and it is this energy that helps the beam exit the laser cylinder straight, narrow, and strong. In business, energy offers the same benefits for individuals, teams, and organizations. Energy and excitement are the fuels for focus.

Laser-focused leaders know how to create the right energy. There's stress, but not an overabundance of bad stress. The workplace contains tension that enables creativity and keeps people thinking about how to make their mark on the desired outcomes. The energy that focus creates is productive unless you are the competition. It's the kinds of energy communities summon to respond to a tragedy or exciting opportunity. You don't have to wait for misfortune to bring out the best in your organization. The next four chapters share ideas, strategies, and specific techniques you can use to turbo-charge the work environment. Really turbo-charge it. Imagine a space that generates engaged employees excited by their mission, but not in a near-burnout, working-too-hard way. Your employees are simultaneously jazzed and at peace. Buzzing and relaxed. Vital and balanced. This excitement is contagious in all the best ways.

Managing energy and engagement is an important concern for leaders. When employees are connected to and interested in their work, they can bring more of themselves to it. If employees suffer from burnout or boredom, they can't offer their best effort. When you focus like a laser beam you tap into and create energy and excitement that makes the workplace buzz and flow. And you can start doing this today—without making any major announcements or setting up a project team to manage the change.

1

KNOW AND FEEL THE POWER OF LASER FOCUS

If you follow every dream, you might get lost.
—Neil Young, "The Painter," from the album *Prairie Wind*

Understand that it's the compelling goal—the vision—that creates the drive, not the other way around. People don't normally drive super-fast when they can't see where they're going. Speeding in heavy fog is foolish.
—Steve Pavlina, "Graduating College in Three Semesters," at StevePavlina.com

In a Nutshell

What does it mean to be focused like a laser beam? Laser-focused leaders use methods that improve their clarity, thinking, and results. Both individuals and organizations can be focused, and the two are linked. Focused leaders often manage focused groups.

Here are six indicators of organizational focus: shared perspective, universally understood drumbeat, relevance of tasks, organization alignment, self-correction, and results. It is critical to know whether you are focused and in what ways you or your organization could benefit from improvements.

Is focus something that happens only for a moment, or is it an over-all way of being? Can both individuals and groups achieve focus? Can you be overwhelmed and focused at the same time? The an-swers to all three questions are both "yes" and "it depends." You can experience a moment of laser focus, a precious time where all philo-sophical planets align to produce mental clarity and resolve. Many of the techniques offered in this book will help you create that kind of intense but momentary focus, but that is not its main purpose. Its main purpose is to maximize long-term performance and satisfac-tion, for which steady and continuous improvement of focus is best.

Individuals focus and, together, the organization focuses. Con-trary to what some senior executives may believe, no company can achieve focus unless each leader and team executes with clarity and velocity. Leaders need to ensure that they focus on what matters most. Scattered and discombobulated leaders cause havoc and con-fusion. Unfocused leaders manage unfocused teams. Within an organization, there may be many pockets of high and low perfor-mance and high and low focus. To succeed, you must be a focused leader with a focused team that produces outstanding results to-gether. You should also serve as a catalyst to improve focus within the company.

You can be simultaneously overwhelmed and focused, but only for a short time. When leaders operate in a state of overwhelm, they respond to urgent tasks first and may not get beyond them. Feeling overwhelmed is perhaps the most debilitating condition a leader can suffer. A vicious cycle of procrastination and reactive fire fight-ing instead of proactive leadership makes the problem worse and worse. Departments, divisions, and even entire companies can suf-fer when leaders operate in overwhelm. Results are late, incom-plete, and inadequate. Stress and frustration shroud the department like a dense wet fog. Haplessly overwhelmed leaders are often fired. The bottom line is that leaders must overcome overwhelm in order to focus and succeed.

On the other hand, being overwhelmed can be good. A tem-porary state of overwhelm, for example, one brought on by a sudden breakthrough, is not cause for alarm and may be wonderfully energizing. If feelings of overwhelm continue for more than two weeks, something needs to be done to improve focus. For example, the Acme Company wants to grow and has pitched long-term proposals to several large clients. If any one of these contracts comes through, it will be a significant gain in business. Acme did such a great job pitching the benefits of its products and services that two companies agreed to sign on for long-term contracts. One of them wants giant anvils and the other wants pianos, both suitable for dropping on unsuspecting roadrunners along remote desert paths. This is great news and in an instant, the company, leaders, and all the employees are overwhelmed. The excitement and pride will enable Acme to get by for a short time, but these changes call for realignment and a reprioritization of what's important. Acme's leaders need to determine how to focus and meet the needs of their growing business. If they don't, employees will begin to burn out and their productivity will fall at the very time it needs to rise.

> *Key Point:* Laser focus is a practice. Leaders can improve focus over time by practicing effective methods that support clarity and results.

Leaders need to know what laser focus looks and feels like. The first and most obvious sign of focus is that everyone knows what's important. Having everyone on board is critical. In most organizations, some people are clear about priorities, but many people feel left out and clueless about what they should be doing and how their work supports the company's priorities. Disconnects can occur between senior and middle management, middle and frontline management, and frontline management and individuals. Some functions are clear while others work from their own sheet music. Why do these gaps in clarity and agreement occur? How and to whom you communicate makes a big difference. The quality of relationships also has an impact on communication. You are likely to communicate more frequently and more clearly with people you like than those you dislike. To achieve laser focus, everyone must understand what's most important. This includes the overall mission, short-term and long-term goals, and priorities.

> *Key Point:* Laser focus = Universally shared vision of what's important.

The second indicator of laser focus is a consistent and shared drumbeat that reverberates throughout the organization. The drumbeat is the speed at which work is or should be flowing. The cadence. The rhythm. The pace of the organization. You might find agreement about what's most important but vastly different interpretations about when it needs to get done. Drumbeat differences can cause finger-pointing, resentment, stress, pressure, and worse. Your team members don't want to be the group that others look down upon nor do they want to feel like the only ones working hard to meet deadlines. Peer leaders often disagree about drumbeat and this is deadly to the organization. Think about a high school dance. As each song changes, dancers adjust their movements to match the drumbeat. People have their own style of dance, but everyone dances to the beat. The same should occur in your organization. The drumbeat might need to change from time to time, but the organization should keep pace and adjust as needed. Some companies will see seasonal differences in the drumbeat.

To achieve laser focus, everyone should be clear about the pace of work needed to produce results. If you get out of synch with the rhythm of the organization, it feels odd, off, and uncomfortable. By contrast, when you are dancing in step with music, it is fun; things feel right. Here's a real example: Along an obscure side street next to a railroad yard on the south side of Seattle, there was once a small Amazon.com distribution center. The shelves of books, videos, and music were emptied and stocked twenty-four hours a day. In the corner of the main open space, hung high on the wall, was a traffic light. The red, yellow, and green light let everyone know how many orders needed to be processed. The green light told people that things were humming along just fine. The yellow light indicated that the orders were starting to back up too much and the red light warned that the plant was in the weeds. The drumbeat changed depending on the color of the traffic light. Supervisors would drop what they were doing to help get shipments processed if the backlog got too large. People revved up and chilled out together like disco dancers. In addition to regular variances, the drumbeat increased during the holiday buying season when all Amazon.com hands packed as many gifts as the people and machines could move.

> *Key Point:* Laser focus = The desired drumbeat is clear and everyone moves in synch with this pace.

The third indicator of laser focus is determined by how people spend their time. To achieve focus, people should be spending time on relevant tasks. This is much more difficult than it sounds because the ways in which leaders define relevance are often cloudy. Many leaders would consider any directionally correct task relevant. This leads to watered-down performance and suboptimization of resources. To achieve laser focus, definitions of relevance need to be narrow.

When you define success, you define relevance, although you might not realize it at the time. If success means doing good work, then any task that is considered good could also be considered relevant. Unfortunately, good tasks are far too numerous for all to be done, so using goodness as a filter is not helpful. How do you ensure that you are doing only those tasks that will make the greatest possible difference? You need to change your definition of success to reflect a higher threshold for relevance. For example, imagine that Sally works for you and she supports several projects. If you defined Sally's success as supporting projects, she could do any task that loosely supports any project and her work would be relevant. What if you changed your definition of success for Sally to *enabling the success of the organization by supporting projects in a way that optimizes their timely completion and success?* Would any task that supports a project be relevant now? No. To achieve laser focus, leaders need to take care when defining success and then ensure people are spending their time in ways that best support the organization's goals.

> *Key Point:* Laser focus = People are spending time on relevant work.

Organization alignment is the fourth indicator of focus. Alignment means that each element of the organization is designed to support the most important company goals. In other words, are you set up for success? Often the answer is emphatically no! As goals and conditions change, you may need to realign the organization to maintain focus. It is difficult to do great work when you regularly fight to make internal processes or systems function at all. The more aligned the organization, the easier it will be for people to do their best work. Poor alignment soaks up physical and mental energy and adds hassle to the workplace. Hassle, rework, inefficiencies, and sluggish progress are all common symptoms of inadequate alignment. The best way to de-hassle the organization and improve efficiencies is to realign it. To align the organization, look at and adjust the following elements if needed: structure, roles, culture, processes, practices, goals, metrics, communication, decision-making processes, technology and systems, workflow, skills, and management practices. Ensure that every organizational element is set up to support what's most important.

> *Key Point:* Laser focus = The organization is aligned.

Laser-focused organizations are self-correcting. This fifth indicator of laser focus relies on the health of the work environment. In a self-correcting organization, employees catch problems before they become large and gnarly. Leaders use lively banter to evaluate opportunities as soon as they emerge. Teams see, discuss, and learn from failures. The only way an organization can maintain focus is by creating an environment where all employees are engaged and help the organization to quickly respond to and learn from changes. Leaders who appreciate and model candid communication will have more responsive teams. You can get a sense for whether your organization is self-correcting by answering the following questions:

- How often is the organization blindsided by problems?
- When a failure or problem occurs, how quickly do you hear about it?
- Does your team see and communicate potential problems before they occur?

Your organization's ability to self-correct will enable it to spend less time reacting and more time working on relevant tasks. Increasing engagement and tuned dialogue will improve your team's motivation and ability to self-correct.

Key Point: Laser focus = The organization is self-correcting.

The sixth indicator of laser focus is results. Focus facilitates and enables success and allows the organization to accomplish its most important goals. Not all results come as a result of focus, however. Companies can get results by doing things the hard way. They can succeed in the short term by driving people beyond their comfort zone. Some leaders get the job done through coercion and pressure. You do not need to focus like a laser beam to achieve results. Remember the Acme Company? Its managers could meet the demand of two new large clients without refocusing their efforts—and given the historical success rate of the company's products, that's probably the pattern they'll choose to follow. The costs of doing this will be high, but it is possible. Results obtained in spite of focus stress the organization and may not last. Who wants to work for this kind of organization? If you run your company and people into the ground, you will suffer high turnover and low morale. This makes every bit of success harder and less pleasant.

Focus is necessary if you want success that does not kill the organization along the way. When you focus like a laser beam you achieve results in a way that makes employees want to stay and contribute. Work is more meaningful and fun. People feel pride in the part they play to support the company's success. Inside the organization there's pride, ownership, and passion that can be felt and seen by customers and competitors.

> *Key Point:* Laser focus = Excellent results with few casualties.

Those are the six indicators of laser focus. How is your organization doing? How focused are you? These indicators should show you why focus is a long-term endeavor and practice. Leaders do many things that affect their and their organization's ability to focus. If you feel like you need help becoming more focused, you are not alone. In a survey of 130 professionals, 87 percent said that focus was very important and 64 percent said it was difficult to achieve. Only 15 percent reported that their department focused well, and 22 percent said their company was focused. And only 15 percent said they were meeting or beating their goals. These professionals said that multiple distractions (a problem of relevance and alignment), too many things to do (a problem of relevance and alignment), and competing or conflicting priorities (a problem of alignment and sharing what's important) were the biggest obstacles to focus.

Obtaining and maintaining focus is not easy. The rest of the book zeros in on methods that will help you improve clarity and results. Focusing is intentional. You cannot just try harder and expect to achieve laser focus. In fact, work should be easier and more fluid. When you choose to focus—really focus—like a laser beam focus—you are releasing a powerful force into the organization. That's right, a force. When the right work flows well, the environment feels different. The positive energy is palpable. You can feel it, and your employees will too.

In the Real World

The six indicators of laser focus can help you determine where improvements are needed. This section offers a chart, a worksheet, and a story to further illustrate these points.

How This Book Addresses the Six Indicators of Focus

As mentioned in the Introduction, this book is organized around three qualities of laser beams and offers ten techniques. You can use these ten techniques to strengthen the indicators of focus. Here's how the ten techniques relate to the six indicators. Each "X" flags a direct link between the technique and building the indicator of focus.

	What's Important Is Shared	Drumbeat Clear	Relevance	Alignment	Self-Correction	Results
Know and feel the power of laser focus	X	X	X	X	X	X
Pump energy into the work environment	X	X	X		X	X
Make work personal	X		X		X	X
Relax to energize			X		X	X
Turn meetings into focus sessions	X	X	X	X	X	X
Invite a challenge			X	X	X	X
Huddle	X	X	X		X	X
Stop multitasking, start chunking	X		X			X
Do one great thing	X	X	X		X	X
Let go	X		X	X		X

Focus Assessment

Take this worksheet to your next staff meeting. Ask the participants how they would assess the organization's focus and suggest the results be used to map needed improvements.

Indicators of Organizational Focus	Needs Improvement	Good	Strength
The mission, goals, and top priorities are known and understood by all employees.			
The desired drumbeat is clear. The desired pace, speed of work, and sense of urgency is known and shared.			
People are spending time on relevant work (that is, on tasks that support what's most important).			
The organization is aligned. We are set up for success. Our structure, roles, systems, and processes optimally support our goals.			
The organization is self-correcting. Problems are caught quickly and failures don't often blindside us.			
We achieve great results without overstressing the organization.			

From the CEO's Perspective

Ken Thrasher is the CEO at Compli, an Oregon-based company that provides compliance management systems. He answered a few questions about focus:

Q: *How do you know when you are focused?*

A: When the team is aligned around a common set of goals and objectives that have measurable results in a time line that is reasonable and you are tracking progress against them. The key word is *alignment*, where teamwork results in all members of the team rowing in the same direction. The focus needs to come from the board and senior management where people understand their role clearly in the mission of the organization.

Q: *How can you tell whether employees are focused?*

A: I read body language and observe people. I can tell by how they react and act. For example, I sometimes see people camping—getting into little groups—and this is a signal there might be a problem or some dysfunction. We need to address those situations quickly or relationships become strained. Deal with it right away. You have to get out to see what's happening. I don't use it to micromanage the organization. I communicate openly with my managers and ensure that people are not surprised to see me as I MBWA [manage by wandering around].

Q: *To what degree do you believe how people feel about their work affects focus?*

A: How people feel impacts focus 100 percent. Our business is built on relationships and knowing our customers. We need to create a positive service orientation and help people with finding solutions that build customer satisfaction and loyalty. I want people to feel comfortable raising their hands if they need help.

Q: *In your experience, what can a leader do to energize the work environment?*

A: It starts with leadership, setting the right environment where employees feel they have a voice in the organization, dealing with environmental issues, and taking time to recognize employees' efforts and do things that are fun. Energy determines output. If employees do not have balance, they cannot do their best work. They are not mentally with you, so focus cannot be achieved. This is critical for senior leaders, too. If anything is out of balance, you cannot manage effectively. A couple of years ago, I discovered I was out of balance physically and spiritually. I started exercising and such, and I felt better in all areas and am a more effective leader.

Q: How much of a challenge is it to ensure that you are spending your time in ways that will benefit the business the most? What techniques or practices help you decide how to spend your time?

A: I'm a big believer in goal setting and being sure I accomplish what I set out to each day. It all has to relate to the strategic plan and what the business is trying to accomplish. I generally determine the day before what I want to accomplish the next day, and make sure things I don't necessarily like to do but must do are on the list. Too often those things that people don't like to do end up on the bottom of the to-do list and never get taken care of, which often leads to dysfunctions in the organization.

Q: Describe how a highly focused day looks and feels.

A: I start by reviewing my goals for the day and make sure they are scheduled around other activities I need to accomplish. I try to get out and talk to a few people in the organization to see how things are going, keep a finger on the pulse of the organization. I step back and think about what we may be missing, how are we doing against our goals, are there weak spots in our plan. Always be prepared for the unexpected, a customer that may be having issues, an employee with personal or business problems that wants to talk to me, or a shareholder that calls with questions. This is where customer service (employee, customer, shareholder) gets differentiated, the ability to respond effectively. When I am focused, I feel accomplishment, clarity, and alignment.

Q: In your organization, what are the greatest barriers to focus?

A: People operating in departmental silos without alignment and understanding what's important for the business. This often costs the organization time, rework, and cost. A previous organization I worked for was big into process analysis and understanding who our customer is, both externally and internally. ECRS was an acronym for eliminate, combine, rearrange, and simplify, and we always first looked at elimination to be sure whatever we were doing added value. The lack of focus often results in doing things with little or no value, or even creating unnecessary costs. This requires constant communication to be effective.

2

GET INTIMATE WITH YOUR EMPLOYEES

We need others. We need others to love and we need to be loved by them. There is no doubt that without it, we too, like the infant left alone, would cease to grow, cease to develop, choose madness and even death.

—Leo Buscaglia, *Love*

My experience suggests that intimacy has two main components: RISK and COMMITMENT. . . . Risk and commitment both require decisions.

—Victor L. Brown Jr., *Human Intimacy*

Oh, the comfort—the inexpressible comfort of feeling safe with a person—having neither to weigh thoughts nor measure words, but pouring them all right out, just as they are, chaff and grain together; certain that a faithful hand will take and sift them, keep what is worth keeping, and then with the breath of kindness blow the rest away.

—Dinah Craik, *A Life for a Life*, 1859

In a Nutshell

Intimate relationships are those where you feel free to be yourself. You can express your feelings and be vulnerable. Leaders who create intimate relationships improve energy, engagement, and focus. You can be both open and professional. To improve relationships, leaders should go first and provide an excellent role model for connection. Employees respect leaders who are open.

To build intimacy, people need to get to know one another on a deep level. Employees want to connect with their managers and feel they are trustworthy. Leaders should show interest in their employees, too. Building and maintaining relationships is necessary for a focused and high-performing team.

◆　◆　◆

HR professionals may rush to read this chapter to ensure that it does not say what they fear; that bosses should have sex with their employees. They can rest easy because the word *sex* appears only three times here (including the two in this paragraph), and this chapter has nothing to do with that kind of intimacy. Nonetheless, it may still seem uncomfortable to discuss business relationships as being intimate. The goal of this chapter is to help you get over this objection and get excited about the benefits of deep work relationships.

What does intimacy mean? How can you tell when a work relationship is intimate? In *The Dance of Intimacy*, Harriet Lerner offers this provoking definition:

> Let's attempt a working definition of an intimate relationship. What does it require of us? For starters, intimacy means that we can be who we are in a relationship, and allow the other person to do the same. . . . An intimate relationship is one in which neither party silences, sacrifices, or betrays the self and each party expresses strength and vulnerability, weakness and competence in a balanced way [1990, p. 3].

An intimate relationship is one where people feel comfortable being themselves. Think about this from a business perspective. As a leader, you want to tap into the intelligence, drive, and uniqueness of each of your employees. You hire people to contribute to the organization, and to make an impact they need to share their thoughts, ideas, and experiences. If you want people to share what they have to offer, you need to create an environment in which doing so is comfortable.

Key Point: People feel comfortable being themselves in intimate relationships. Leaders need to tap into and apply the talent they have hired.

To feel comfortable, your employees need to receive the same level of sharing and generosity from you. You can't ask people to take risks, be vulnerable, and open themselves up for criticism and not offer the same. Leaders who deal with people openly and generously will encourage and reinforce the same behavior from others. In *Management of the Absurd,* Richard Farson writes about the importance of vulnerability in building relationships:

> Absurdly, our most important human affairs—marriage, child rearing, education, leadership—do best when there is occasional loss of control and an increase in personal vulnerability, times when we do not know what to do. . . . Managers think the people with whom they work want them to exhibit consistency, assertiveness, and self-control—and they do, of course. But occasionally, they also want just the opposite. They want a moment with us when we are genuinely ourselves without façade or pretense or defensiveness, when we are revealed as human beings, when we are vulnerable [1996, p. 38].

Here is a true story about two vice presidents. Both were smart and caring men. John's team loved working for and with him. They felt connected to their work and were energetic about helping the function improve. Michael, who in many ways was smarter and more creative than John, suffered from high turnover on his team. Many people did not enjoy working for Michael and they did not feel connected to their work. Both managed in the same department and worked with many of the same people. The key difference was their ability to create and nurture intimate relationships. John was open and appreciated candid feedback from his team members. He sometimes showed his vulnerability. Michael spoke to people as though they were machines and did not welcome criticism or candor. Although John did not have as many ideas as Michael, John's team outthought and outcreated Michael's team by a long shot. John's team was more focused and successful because of the way in which team members related to one another.

Key Point: Leaders need to model intimacy and show their more human side to optimize focus, energy, and results.

John knew that connected, deep, intimate relationships improved results, but he also valued the way this openness influenced his employees' work life. It is more fun, more meaningful, and more compelling to work in an environment that is intimate. With one third or more of your day spent at work, it is critical to spend all this time in a way that is satisfying.

Perhaps you are thinking that you prefer to keep business and personal relationships separate. But you do not need to go bowling with your employees to develop business intimacy. You can be both open and focused on the business. You can be professional and intimate. Frankly, the "let's keep it professional" argument is a cop-out. Some leaders have a hard time being real, being open, and showing who they really are to their employees. These leaders are not getting close enough to learn from or tap into the most amazing talents their team has to offer.

Leaders need to get over their fear and discomfort and get real with their employees, peers, and managers. Why does this fear exist? Many think that showing weaknesses or admitting mistakes will reduce the respect people have for them and diminish their leadership power. Here's the thing, though—if you're a leader, your people *already know* your strengths and weaknesses. If you are defensive to criticism, everyone knows this. If analysis is not your strong suit, everyone knows this. If you are cranky in the mornings or hate being challenged in front of your boss, people have seen this. Being open about your feelings and honest about setbacks will not diminish your capability to lead—it will increase it. People respect leaders who acknowledge their developmental needs and share their struggles. Leaders who develop deep, connecting relationships are much more powerful because people follow them willingly, not because of their title or position.

Key Point: Employees respect leaders who are open about failures or setbacks. Intimate business relationships enhance a leader's power.

Keith Ferrazzi Suggests Dialogue Goes Deep Fast

Keith Ferrazzi, author of *Never Eat Alone,* suggests that leaders should move with lightning speed past the idle chitchat and dive into the topics that mean something.

> Too many people confuse secrecy with importance. Business schools teach us to keep everything close to our vest. But the world has changed. Power, today, comes from sharing information, not withholding it. More than ever, the lines demarcating the personal and professional have blurred. We're an open-source society, and that calls for open-source behavior. And as a rule, not many secrets are worth the energy required to keep them secret. Being up front with people confers respect; it pays them the compliment of candor [2005, p. 145].

Go deep fast. Real connections are intimate. Meaningful conversations are intimate. To be most effective, we need to take more risks and share how we feel and think about important business problems. Committed work is personal, not superficial.

What does being open mean? How do leaders nurture intimacy? The three chapters in Part Two offer techniques for improving intimacy in everyday conversations. Before these recommendations for tuned dialogue will work, however, your employees will need to feel that they know you and can trust you. Your team members want to know what's important to you, your beliefs about work, and what (related to the business) keeps you up at night. They want to know what you value and they want to learn your idiosyncrasies. Your employees are interested in getting to know you because you make an enormous difference to their experience at work. Working for a great boss is enjoyable and satisfying. Getting stuck with a lousy boss can leave the most interesting work feeling more like drudgery. Even so, even unenlightened leaders can benefit from letting their employees get to know them. When people know you, they are more likely to look past minor annoyances (everyone has them) and help you succeed.

Trustworthiness is another matter. If you are not trustworthy, you will have trouble engaging your team, and both focus and results will suffer. Trust is a funny thing. Here's the irony about leadership trustworthiness. While being trustworthy is critical, it is also the easiest leadership trait to model. Being trustworthy is simple, simple, simple. All you need to do is keep your promises, be honest, represent your people's needs, and never badmouth people behind their backs.

Nonetheless, even though trust should be easy to attain, it is often lacking. When employees feel they cannot trust you, they hold back because they don't want to get burned for caring about the business. Intimacy and trust feed each other. When you trust someone, you share yourself. When you share yourself, you build trust.

> *Key Point:* To build intimacy, leaders need to be trustworthy and allow employees to get to know them.

You will also want to show interest in getting to know your employees. What makes them tick? What fuels their work passions? Do they have any pet peeves? Why have they chosen this job and what are their goals? When was the last time they had a great day and why was it great? Sharing stories and dreams fuels deep relationships.

Here is a true story. Eileen was a vice president and a department head. She had technical knowledge but was a poor leader of people. She'd been promoted based on her functional expertise and her assertiveness. Nobody liked working for her. That's not a strong enough statement. *People hated working for Eileen.* She seemed to have no interest in her people and gave them little attention or thought. People felt she did not care and she made no attempt to know anything about them. Eileen was not a conversationalist. The mediocre workers stayed and worked below their capacity. The top talent quickly left.

This case is extreme, but it brings up an important point. Some leaders honestly have no interest in getting to know their people. They just don't feel a need to know anything beyond how someone performs assigned work. Why do companies tolerate this? This logic would not be accepted in other aspects of the business. Imagine a high-tech manufacturing plant filled with state-of-the-art machinery. This machinery needs to be maintained and tuned to optimize and sustain output. What would happen if output suffered because a leader ignored the equipment and it was not maintained? That leader would be fired and out on the street!

The common rhetoric is always true, whether or not those who use it actually mean it: people really are a company's greatest and often most expensive resource. They need to be maintained and cared for or output will suffer. Building strong and deep relationships should not be an option; it should be a basic requirement for all leaders. When employees do not feel connected to either their manager or the company, they may focus more on what's wrong than on how to help the company meet its goals. What people focus on is a choice. If you want your people to choose to focus on the business, help them feel connected to it.

> *Key Point:* Showing interest in your people is a basic leadership requirement to ensure focus and results.

Leadership expert Chip Bell wrote about the benefits of intimacy in a Fall 2005 *Leader to Leader* article, "The Vulnerable Leader."

What is the greatest payoff of leading with vulnerability? In a phrase: unbridled passion. Passion is not something leaders give, it is something they release. As leaders publicly connect with their true selves, they issue an implied invitation for followers to do likewise. Heads do not talk to hearts; only hearts talk to hearts [2005, p. 23].

Take another look at the definition of intimacy. It's a relationship where both parties feel comfortable being themselves. Wouldn't anyone prefer that freedom? When you can be yourself, you feel relaxed, engaged, and happier. You bring more of yourself to work—more energy, more creativity, more discipline. More intensity, more passion, more ownership. To be focused like a laser beam, you and your team need to be jazzed about your work and about one another.

In the Real World

Are you convinced of the virtues of building intimate work relationships? This section discusses ways to spark connection and nurture mutual interest.

Ways to Build Intimacy

Intimacy occurs in communication. When two or more people share from their hearts and minds, they relate in a deep way. Here are several suggestions you can use to get closer to your employees and peers:

- Skip the weather and ask people about how they feel.
- Be inclusive in conversations; don't leave people out. Sure, it is not appropriate to invite everyone to all meetings, but be aware of the people you connect with informally, and spread the contact around.
- Touch on various topics during one-on-ones and check in with your employees to see how the job and work is going for them.

- Share your core beliefs. Create a list headed "What I Believe In," and share it with your employees, manager, and peers. Talk about your beliefs and how they affect your leadership style.

- Ask your employees for coaching. Talking to your employees about the areas in which you want to develop will make them more comfortable discussing the same with you.

- Practice open-book management. Share company information, department measures and results, and the company's goals. Invite your employees to contribute to developing departmental goals.

- Be honest, open, and direct with employees when their performance is lacking. They need to trust that if you have not told them otherwise, things are fine.

- Spend time with your employees doing off-site activities like lectures, a field trip, or a quarterly off-site lunch.

- Get to know each other's natural behavioral tendencies. Ask the OD or training department to facilitate a session where you each take and share your behavioral styles using an assessment like the Myers-Briggs Type Indicator. Getting to know each other's natural preferences and behavioral pet peeves is fun and helpful.

- Practice extreme listening (described in the next section).

Extreme Listening

You've heard of active listening, right? To create intimacy, go beyond active listening and give extreme listening a try. Think about someone you admire. For example, Gandhi. Imagine you are going to meet with Gandhi and he is going to share his vision of a free India with you. As you listen, you find yourself staring at him. You hang on every word he says. You are in the presence of greatness and you feel blessed and special. You would not think of interrupting Gandhi, and you are present with him. In other words, you are just listening, hearing, taking his words in; you are not thinking about what you will say next. This conversation is not about you—it is about Gandhi.

Now imagine that your employee Sue is like Gandhi. She is amazing. Give her your undivided attention just as you would someone you admire a great deal. Hang on her every word and just be present to the conversation. If you find that your thoughts start wandering or skipping ahead to what you will say, wrangle them back. This time is for Sue. Look her in the eye often.

When you really hear someone, you get to know them in a much deeper way. You learn the ways in which they are amazing and you will find that your admiration increases. Try extreme listening at least once a day for a week and notice what happens. Your conversations will be better and your relationships will build. Extreme listening is a gift for you and your employees.

Show Your 31 Flavors

In *The Likeability Factor*, Tim Sanders suggests you identify your "31 Flavors," or words that describe your uniqueness. The flavors are broken down as follows:

- Seven words that describe the way you are on normal days
- Six words that describe you when you are fully engaged and at your best
- Six words that describe you when you are at your worst
- Six words that describe people you admire
- Six words that a friend would use to describe you

Sanders suggests you write down the list of words on a piece of paper then select ten words that best state who you really are (Sanders, 2005, p. 193). Share this information with your team or do this as a team activity. It is a fun and illuminating way to get to know one another better and on a deeper level.

Sanders also suggests that all leaders should improve their likeability, or what he calls the L-Factor, to build positive work relationships. In addition to the suggestions offered in the book, you can take a free likeability assessment on his Web site, www.timsanders.com.

Get Naked

In *Sex, Intimacy and Business*, Lindsay Andreotti and Brian Hilgendorf espouse "getting naked" at work.

> Getting naked, in the context of business, also means bringing the very authentic you into the workplace. Do not cover up the bits you think are not acceptable to unveil at work, or that you are afraid others might not like or understand. Do not worry about the less-than-perfect parts of your personality or behavioral anatomy. That's like hiding your tender bits in the locker room. Why bother? Everyone has them! [2006, p. 49].

Andreotti and Hilgendorf offer three steps to getting naked at work:

- *Create empathy:* Take the time and care to listen to people and see things from their point of view. When you empathize, you acknowledge another person's reality.
- *Align individuals to the company:* Get to know people on a deep level. Understand their desires, goals, passions, and pet peeves and connect these to the goals and mission of the company.
- *Collaborate:* Make collaboration an open, deliberate, and regular practice. Focus on what's most important and use collaboration instead of competition to enliven creativity and focus.

3

HAVE FUN AND BE FUN

Shared joy is a double joy; shared sorrow is half a sorrow.

—Swedish Proverb

Failure is more frequently from want of energy than want of capital.

—Daniel Webster

In a Nutshell

Any job can and should be fun. Employees want their managers to be fun and they want to enjoy their work. Leaders should strive to have fun while doing great work. Fun and focus can be altogether compatible. Having fun should heighten productivity. You want your employees to enjoy doing the most important work because they will do it better.

There are many ways to be fun and have fun at work. Laughing and telling stories is an obvious way to add fun to the day. Other ways include offering challenging problems to solve, giving everyone a fair shot at pleasurable assignments, celebrating successes, and being playful. People will have more fun when they play an active role on a winning team. Having fun can be therapeutic, enabling employees to handle stress better.

You can improve teamwork, engagement, fun, and focus by practicing techniques from improvisational theater. The methods that enable a group of performers to generate an amazing and entertaining story in front of the audience's astonished faces can help you build excitement and creativity at work.

◆ ◆ ◆

Barry raised both hands in the air and let out a cheer. Several months of work had paid off. The new machine was up and running. Thirty feet high and a city block long, the paper-making machine was doing its job. Its gray skin looked beautiful and its hum was like music to his ears. Milky water went in one end and paper came out the other. Several processes quickly turned the fiber slurry into a large, smooth white roll. Amazing! As Barry looked into each section of the machine through safety glass cutouts, he smiled. Then he went over to the fancy controller panel. All indications were positive. Barry was having a great day and he made sure everyone around him knew it. The machine was powerful but paled in comparison to the positive human energy Barry released. His enthusiasm was infectious and the atmosphere was fun.

Fun? Can paper making be fun? Sure! Any job and any business can be fun. Conversely, recreation-based jobs like playing professional sports or leading a group of hikers can be no fun at all. Whether you have fun at work is all in your head. Employees want their managers to be fun and they want to enjoy their work. People choose to focus. They choose to engage in their work. And the best talent will choose to work in an environment that is fun.

How would you like to work as a grocery store cashier or manager? Most people would not consider the grocery business one built on fun and excitement, but fun is at the core for at least one company. Trader Joe's has built a reputation with employees and customers for being a fun place. Employees wear Hawaiian shirts and are empowered to provide excellent customer service. Trader Joe's creates an environment that is cool, friendly, and warm, and its stores sell great stuff. The employees love it and show this with hard work and loyalty. In a labor market often crippled by strikes, Trader Joe's enjoys low turnover and high morale. Having fun is an important part of its mission because its leaders want their intelligent and discerning (but not snobby) clientele to have fun while they shop (Lewis, 2005, pp. 55, 146).

Key Point: Any kind of work, including yours, can and should be fun. Employees vote with their minds and feet.

Having fun does not replace doing great work. In the opening example, Barry was having fun while excelling on the job. Trader Joe's knows that having fun improves sales and profits. Serious fun is great fun. Birthday cakes and Dilbert comics are nice, but they are not the reasons people love their jobs. Having fun while getting into a project is a rush that fuels focus and results. Many leaders pooh-pooh having fun because they believe that it gets in the way of productivity. Don't be one of these ill-informed leaders. You can be fun and focused. Fun and professional. Fun and resolute. Fun with high expectations.

In fact, the more critical the project, the more important it is to have fun with it. People want to be a part of the company's success and can take priority work seriously while enjoying the experience of shaping the present and future. It is an honor to be a part of making the company great. You want your employees to enjoy doing the most important work. If work is also fun, employees bring more of themselves to each task. When people say, "I love my job," they are saying that this important work is meaningful and fun.

Key Point: Important assignments should also be fun.

What does being fun mean? Traditional definitions say that fun makes you laugh, gives you pleasure, or is amusing. How does this translate to work? While some leaders are funny at times, many don't have a witty sense of humor. That's OK; there are other ways to have fun. Some tasks are more pleasurable than others. Leaders can make sure that everyone has an opportunity to participate in pleasurable assignments, but there are still other ways to have fun. Challenging the mind and engaging it in learning can be fun, too. Leaders should encourage learning and stimulating conversations. And there are more ways to have fun. Sometimes it is not the work but the way you go about the work that makes it fun. Are meetings light, upbeat, and fast paced? Playful leaders have more fun and are more fun. Play is important and can be incorporated into most projects and tasks. And winning can be a lot of fun. People enjoy being a part of a winning team. Teams that celebrate successes enjoy the fruits of their labor. Leaders can do many things to have fun and be fun. You can make each day fun by focusing on and sharing your passions and being light-hearted.

> *Key Point:* There are lots of ways to have fun at work. Leaders can be fun to work with and still be focused on the business.

Having fun is therapeutic. Employees are barraged with deadlines, e-mail, phone calls, last-minute requests, and dramatic paper jams. Taking a couple of moments to release that stress and laugh is healthy. Positive energy enlivens the mind and body, counteracting the draining effects of stress and aggravation. The three o'clock coffee break might be the key to your afternoon productivity. So enjoy it!

It can be doubly advantageous to learn to giggle at minor frustrations. When people take the wrong things too seriously, these small events can get in the way of their ability to focus on what's important. A colossal paper jam can ruin someone's day and productivity. By contrast, if they can laugh at it, the event can lighten the day and turn the jam into confetti. Giggling at the silly little things that go wrong does not mean these problems should not be solved, either. Everyone suffers countless tiny failure incidents that are best laughed off—while being fixed before they turn into big failure incidents.

The same can be said for coworker habits that drive you a bit crazy. Learn to love people's idiosyncrasies and never let them ruin your day. If someone is incompetent, this is another issue—and not something to laugh at. That said, you should not get upset over little habits like an annoying laugh or a habit of humming while concentrating. Lee gets his words a bit mixed up. Sarah loses her train of thought in the middle of her sentences. Billy talks too loud. Melanie wears enough perfume for the whole office. After several demonstrations, George still can't figure out how to operate the copier. Tim barges into conversations like a rhino. Cathy falls asleep in meetings. These things can drive you crazy or become the character of the organization. You have habits like these, too, by the way.

> *Key Point:* Moments of fun help provide balance to a stressful day.

How spontaneous is your work environment? Are team conversations mentally stimulating? Being stimulated is fun. Teams that practice improvisational theater (improv), techniques can jack up their ability to work together and imbue the environment with energy, appreciation, and creativity. Improv exercises and games encourage open and fluid thinking.

Improv is amazing to watch. It looks as though it has no rules, no structure, and you wonder how this performance, this collective being, can be happening. No one knows what is going to happen, not even the performers. That's quite extraordinary, really. This group of performers has not predetermined the story they will create. Together they have ventured on the journey and each player is committed and out there—out there emotionally and physically. Each player is fully engaged and astoundingly supportive of all the rest. This is symbiosis in action. There is no glory or reward for individual actions; the story is team generated and propelled.

When you watch improv, you witness extreme teamwork in action. That's right, teamwork. You get the sense that each player has deep respect and appreciation for the others. And they share the responsibility of keeping the story moving. They must; the performance depends on how well the group works together. *The performance depends on how well the group works together.* Sound familiar? It should come as no surprise that using improv techniques in business can enliven and enrich teams. Conversations become more playful and creative. In *Improv Wisdom* (2005), Patricia Ryan Madson wrote: "Improvising invites us to lighten up and look around. It offers an alternative to the controlling way many of us try to lead our lives. It requires that we say yes and be helpful rather than argumentative; it offers us a chance to do things differently" (p. 20).

The improv performance seems devoid of structure, but it isn't. Several underlying principles help guide player creativity and actions. These principles are agreements about how they will work together. "The invitation to improvise is not a prescription for a careless approach to life" (Madson, 2005, p. 24). When business teams practice improv techniques, they explore their ability to generate together. An effective and energizing way to pump up energy, fun, and teamwork is to practice improv techniques. A team that thinks and acts well together is more focused and productive.

> *Key Point:* Use improvisation to improve team function, thinking, and fun.

People want to have fun at work and they will gravitate toward what's fun. As a leader you have a choice. Make work fun, or become the subject of your people's water cooler jokes. Leaders who are fun and have fun drench the work environment in positive energy that enables focus and success.

In the Real World

Ready to have some fun and energize your workplace? Even the most conservative and stodgy leader can promote a work environment where people have fun.

Twenty Ways to Have Fun at Work

In *301 Ways to Have Fun at Work,* Dave Hemsath and Leslie Yerkes write: "We believe that fun at work may be the single most important trait of a highly effective and successful organization; we see a direct link between fun at work and employee creativity, productivity, morale, satisfaction, and retention, as well as customer service and many other factors that determine business success" (1997, p. viii).

Hemsath and Yerkes offer hundreds of ideas for having fun at work. Here are just a few:

- Don't take yourself too seriously. Make sure you are not the source of stress.
- Do at least one thing that brings you joy each day.
- Listen to upbeat music when doing simple tasks.
- Impose flashy shirt Friday.
- Bring candy to meetings. Have chocolate kisses in a jar on your desk.
- Encourage employees to personalize their work areas.
- Hire great team members.
- Energetically appreciate great work.
- Use an internal blog to heighten informal communication.
- Smile.
- Play brain-stimulating games to warm up a meeting.
- Have brief weekly team development sessions.
- Brainstorm ideas.
- Hold meetings outside.
- Think from different perspectives.
- Get involved in supporting local charities together—like a walk-a-thon.
- Have a potluck.
- Make the work environment a pleasing place to work.
- Show your true personality.
- Encourage employees to express their interests and passions.

Having fun is a chosen state of mind. Once you decide to have more fun at work, the opportunities to energize yourself and your team are endless. You can do simple things that mean a lot to your people. Even if you are a bit uncomfortable at first, that's OK. Your team will see that you are making an effort and will reward you with their thanks and performance.

Try Improvisation

Consultant and improv practitioner Johnnie Moore has helped companies build team energy and creativity using improv exercises. The connection between what's created in the theater and the benefits for business teams is logical.

"What theatrical improvisors do is quite remarkable," Moore says. "They show the audience a very high form of teamwork. Improv principles are simple and powerful. While you can read about improv techniques in a book, you won't learn much about it until you do it. It is a learn-by-doing thing. If you engage in the activities, you can feel their power and applicability to teamwork."

The exercises call for participants to take a risk, to venture into the unknown. Moore recommends that your initial foray into improv be facilitated by a qualified consultant who has used improv in a business setting and can guide you through the learning process. This is important for two reasons. First, people react differently to improv exercises and some people will need guidance and support. Second, you will want to participate with your team.

Using improv will help you develop more playful relationships and put people in a space where more things are possible. Team members become more able to create within a set of constraints. Moore says: "Most of us see constraints as very limiting. But the truth is that constraints can stimulate creativity. Some people look at improv and see it as anarchy, but they are missing the point. There are constraints and rules that improve creativity. You explore the inventive ways you can create within the constraints."

Moore recommends the following schedule for your initial exploration of improv techniques:

- Hold five facilitated workshops two or three hours long.
- Schedule the workshops a week or two apart.
- Start with an introductory session if you are unsure about how your team will take to improv.
- Go to www.johnniemoore.com or www.appliedimprov.net for more information, to read articles, or find an improv practitioner.

If you want to explore teamwork on a new level, try improv. With each practice, your team will improve their ability to collaborate and create great results together. With improv, team members form more dynamic and engaging relationships and might actually be surprised at what they can achieve together.

Example Improv Exercise

"Yes, And" is a powerful improv principle. In this example, from an essay called "Simple Ideas, Lightly Held," Johnnie Moore offers an exercise that will build team affirmation and appreciation:

Yes, And

At its simplest level, this is an injunction to stop saying "No, but" to our colleagues and instead say "Yes, and." It's not always going to work, but I've been surprised at the difference it makes when I find myself able to do this with sincerity. No, I'm not suggesting that you simply agree with everything people say to you, so don't panic. To put this all in context, here's another simple activity you could try with a colleague.

What I Like . . .

Pick a subject where you'd like to generate a few creative ideas. For a warm-up, maybe choose one that's not of world-shattering importance, so that it's easy to engage with lightness. Like . . . where shall we go for lunch next time?

The first person gets to make one suggestion for what you do—say, "Let's go to the staff cafeteria."

The second person then says, "Yes, what I like about that idea is . . . " and then adds something they do like about it. The challenge is to find something you really like, which may take a second or two. For example "Yes, what I like about that idea is that it's a quick journey and that means we can spend more time talking."

This person then continues, "And we could—" making another suggestion. For this exercise, don't worry too much about connecting to the first idea, just play. So you might say, "And we could eat the hottest curry on the menu."

Back to the first person, who now continues with "Yes, what I like about that idea is . . . that as I don't eat spicy food, I get to do most of the talking!"

And so on, until you decide to stop for coffee.

What this exercise may bring up:

For a lot of folks, this is great fun; they generate some wild ideas and get enthusiastic. Others play at a slower pace but learn that they can find things to appreciate in what another person says, if they try.

And a few hate it, because (they say) it forces fake enthusiasm. That's an interesting point of view, but I don't believe the activity forces that—it's a choice the participants make. With an effort I think it's always possible to find something to appreciate about the other's offer.

I'd observe that within the structure of this activity, people will explore what's possible and therefore come up with different styles and interpretations. That's why I tend to ask people to play games without attempting to explain what "the point is."

Anyway, some will insist on No, Butting a Yes, And activity. And No, But is always an option. Generally, I've found Yes, Anding works well for me in many more cases because most people like to be acknowledged.

The Simple Power of Acknowledgment . . .

"Yes, And" is sometimes more about acknowledgment of the other than it is about agreement. I think acknowledging other people's experience can be remarkably powerful, especially in situations of conflict. Yet it's something we as a race are incredibly bad at doing. What we like to do is offer our interpretation of what someone tells us, or rush to suggestions on how to avoid having certain feelings, rather than simply acknowledging them. Time and again, I find that when I stop and simply let someone know I've heard what they said, and the way they said it, the quality of conversation improves for both of us. And when others do it to me, the impact is similarly strong.

And I've done it for myself. I remember on September 12, 2001, I was talking to an old friend who had invited me over for lunch. I actually felt unable to leave home, suffering like many other people from the shock of the day before. And then I just said to him, "Oh, I realize I feel too afraid to go out of the door, just give me a minute or two to feel that." And after a few moments of acknowledging this fear, I soon felt quite happy to go on the visit [Moore, 2005, p. 80].

4

RELAX TO ENERGIZE

Saying "yes" to more things than we can actually manage to be present for with integrity and ease of being is in effect saying "no" to all those things and people and places we have already said "yes" to.

—Jon Kabat-Zinn, *Coming to Our Senses*

In a Nutshell

Many leaders have such hectic days that they are too frazzled to think and too tired to exercise. This can be a vicious cycle. Too much stress kills focus and productivity. You likely know that stress is an internal biochemical response, but do you know how to combat stress? The antidote is relaxation. Leaders need to learn to relax to focus like a laser beam.

Many work environments reinforce the wrong behavior by rewarding action that leads to burnout. Many leaders feel too self-conscious to practice relaxation at work. Get over it! The focus and success of your department depends on everyone's ability to think clearly and well. Begin practicing quick-and-easy relaxation techniques and encourage your team members to do the same.

Exhausted, you awake to an angry-sounding alarm clock. Coffee gets you going enough to make it out the door on time. During the morning commute you zone out, oblivious to the radio's barrage of the latest war casualties. At work, juggling your cell phone, landline, BlackBerry, and e-mail, you speak to countless faceless people all without leaving your desk. For lunch, you find something from a vending machine and eat hunched over a pile of paperwork. You are too tired to exercise. It's fall, but the color of the leaves goes unnoticed as you race home. By day's end you're back where you started and all you've gained is a headache.

Daily stress, and the fatigue and strain that it causes, kills focus and productivity. The hectic, busy lifestyle of most professionals zaps the energy they need to excel. Being driven is wonderful, but you need to be aware of and manage the pitfalls of go-go-going. Education scientist (and head of the Association for Holistic Learning) Charmaine Liebertz offered this warning in the October 2005 issue of *Scientific American Mind:*

> At some point, such driven people are likely to hit the wall. Their built-up tensions will be unleashed on some unfortunate, unsuspecting person. Or they will find themselves in the hospital with a bleeding ulcer or heart palpitations. At a minimum, they will become less effective thinkers, defeating their very ability to accomplish mental tasks. Constant scrambling and extreme workloads may bring success short-term, but the long-term, negative effects are serious [p. 88].

Laser-focused leaders are able to keep the pace of work brisk while taking care of their ability to think and create.

Key Point: A stressful, busy, and hectic work pace causes many professionals to lose focus and energy.

Most people know and acknowledge that stress is an internal biochemical response that occurs as a response to changes in the environment. Each individual will respond to a given set of stimuli differently. Some drivers find heavy traffic stressful, while others take it in stride.

The antidote to negative stress is relaxation. Relaxation is also an internal response and one that can reduce the negative effects of stress and improve thinking and focus.

Here's the irony. Many work environments positively reinforce behaviors that produce negative stress, which in turn hinders focus and results. Few companies encourage leaders to improve relaxation, which improves focus and results. This notion—that a frenetic pace is good and taking five minutes to calm your mind is bad—has to go! This thinking is backwards and will harm your health, satisfaction, and ability to perform—and your team members' too.

> *Key Point:* Stress is an internal response. To improve focus, leaders should address and counteract this internal response by using relaxation techniques throughout their busy day.

You do not need to retreat for a month to an ancient village in the Himalayas to learn to relax (though that sounds like fun). You do not need to sign up for evening yoga classes attended by people who transform into human pretzels (though yoga classes are very beneficial). To relax your mind, you do not need to bring ylang-ylang incense to work and sit in the lotus position and chant. Perhaps one reason leaders do not do more to relax is that they feel the techniques are too far outside the mainstream of business. Maybe they feel embarrassed or self-conscious about taking five or ten minutes to reflect quietly. Might the problem be that the work environment would call leaders who relax *lax* or *slackers?* Given what's at risk, this is just crazy!

As a leader, you can break the destructive cycle of reinforcing the wrong behaviors and beliefs. The focus and success of your department depends on everyone's ability to think clearly and well. Relaxation techniques do not have to look new-agey and they can be incorporated into everyone's busy day. Be a positive role model by improving your relaxation and by sharing the techniques that you find work best in your work environment. If several leaders and teams point the way, practicing relaxation will become part of the culture.

> *Key Point:* Many relaxation techniques take just a few minutes and deliver big benefits during the workday.

Leaders should encourage employees to take a couple of brief relaxation breaks each day and as situations warrant. Talk about focus and mental clarity during meetings and informal conversations. Provide your team with resources and information that will help them learn how to relax their minds. Encourage afternoon mini power walks. Share articles, books, and DVDs that you find helpful.

Another way you can reinforce the right behaviors is by respecting your employees' privacy when they are taking a mental break. With most employees working in loud cubicle villages or open work environments, it is a challenge to relax. Be flexible and allow employees to listen to music through headphones or get out of the office for brief periods of time. Be sure that you do not inadvertently make your staff feel guilty for taking a break.

> *Key Point:* To ensure your team can focus and do their best work, encourage employees to take brief, stress-reducing breaks.

Being mindful means paying attention in a particular way. Mindfulness is the practice whereby you make yourself intentionally aware of your thoughts and actions in the present moment. When you are mindful, you are alert in a way that is nonreactive and nonjudgmental.

Jon Kabat-Zinn, a well-respected stress cessation authority, has spent more than twenty-five years studying the human relationship with anxiety. He is the founding director of the Stress Reduction

Clinic and the Center for Mindfulness in Medicine, Health Care, and Society at the University of Massachusetts Medical School, as well as professor emeritus of medicine. In *Coming to Our Senses* (2005), Kabat-Zinn describes the power of mindfulness:

> Of all the meditative wisdom practices that have developed in traditional cultures throughout the world and throughout history, mindfulness is perhaps the most basic, the most powerful, the most universal, among the easiest to grasp and engage in, and arguably, the most sorely needed now. For mindfulness is none other than the capacity we all already have to know what is actually happening as it is happening [p. 109].

Mindfulness gives rise to awareness and insight that you can cultivate by paying attention. You can refine your ability to be mindful by practicing mindfulness meditation. Don't let the word *meditation* cause you alarm. Meditation means entering a state in which you relax your body and calm and focus your mind. There are many simple ways to meditate.

> *Key Point:* Paying attention helps the mind relax and focus.

One of the most important things to pay attention to is your breath. The quality of your breathing influences your mental and physical energy and wellness. Many people do not breathe well, particularly at work. As leaders rush from one task to another, many develop a pattern of breathing that is short and shallow. Some people hold their breath many times an hour! Dennis Lewis, author of *Free Your Breath, Free Your Life*, offers this about breathing:

> Few of us in today's stress-filled world breathe in a free, natural, and harmonious way. Our mostly flat, constricted breathing undermines our physical, emotional, and spiritual health and well-being, and deprives us, without our even knowing it, of one of the great joys of living on this earth: the expansive sensation of a free, easy, boundless

breath that engages the whole of ourselves and connects us with all of life [2004, p. 1].

Breathing is the foundation of many practices that improve calmness and mental clarity, including yoga, tai chi, and meditation. To begin benefiting from better breathing, you should seek to become more aware of your breath. This is called conscious breathing and you can start by taking a few minutes throughout the day to be present to how you are breathing and to notice the air as it travels in and out of your body. Don't think too much about it or try to force a visualization. Just breathe and be aware of the inner and outer sensations of your breath. Professional athletes work on their breathing and know that it influences their performance. Breathing also influences business performance. When you breathe well, you improve your focus and mental clarity and feed your brain, senses, and body.

> *Key Point:* Many people do not breathe well. To fuel your brain and body, practice better breathing.

Your ability to focus like a laser beam depends on your ability to think clearly and well. Leaders who allow themselves to become overwhelmed and stressed out will suffer from a frazzled mind. Like many things at work, the stress rolls downhill. If you are distracted, your team will likely feel the same. When you and your team members practice relaxation techniques throughout the day, you will enjoy improved focus, enjoyment, and performance.

In the Real World

You have many options for adding relaxation techniques to your busy day. Find and practice methods that you enjoy and that fit best into your day. Many people are surprised by the effectiveness of simple relaxation techniques. Here is a diverse list of ideas you can try, followed by a real-life story.

Office Yoga

Darrin Zeer has been teaching leaders and organizations yoga for more than fifteen years. His work has been profiled on CNN and he has worked with companies such as 3M, Pixar, and Four Seasons Resorts. In *Office Yoga*, Zeer offers many simple stretches that can be done while at the office. He also recommends relaxation practices to perform at home. This small and friendly book offers a great introduction to many stretches that you and your employees can use to improve focus. Zeer says that people lose access to their intelligence when overwhelmed. If you are stressed out it is hard to do simple tasks, let alone make an important decision. And the problem is worse now than ever. Thanks to technology advancements, you may never feel off the job. The seven-days-per-week-always-plugged-in work culture makes it tough to quiet your thoughts and give your mind and body a chance to relax. Zeer recommends leaders practice the art of being calm.

> I worry that people have a negative connotation of the word *relax*. *Calm* might be a better word. It is a powerful word. When I am calm, I can tap into a power beyond my own. Be calm and the intelligence will come. When you are not calm, it is like temporary insanity. Suppressing your thoughts and pretending to be calm is not calm. When you achieve calm, magic happens.

Zeer also stresses the importance of breathing to cut physical and mental stress. When relaxing on vacation, you take nice long and relaxed breaths. In the office, many people shorten or hold their breath. If you take just a few deep breaths, you short-circuit the stress response. That's all it takes; five long, deep breaths. Here are two office stretches that Darrin recommends for improving focus and mental clarity:

- The Kick Back Log-on Pose: Interlace your fingers behind your head. Relax your elbows and shoulders. Smile, breathe, and stretch your elbows back. Let the tightness release slowly. Repeat throughout the day [Zeer, 2000, p. 30].

- E-mail Meditation: While you are reading e-mail, remember to breathe slowly and focus your attention on your breath. Make the out-breath two times longer than the in-breath. This will immediately calm you [Zeer, 2000, p. 34].

These stretches reverse some of the tension caused by sitting at a desk all day. Yoga is a five-thousand-year-old science dedicated to strengthening, revitalizing, and calming your body and mind. When you are under the gun at work (and who isn't?), you need all the help you can get. You need to support yourself to succeed. Try these two exercises or others found in *Office Yoga*.

Breakout for Brain Power

Herbert Benson is the founder of the Mind/Body Medical Institute and an associate professor of medicine at Harvard Medical School. He has researched the effects of stress on thinking for more than thirty-five years. In *The Breakout Principle*, Benson recommends that professionals try these four steps to improve their ability to focus their minds and solve problems:

1. Struggle to solve an important problem or complex task. Concentrate, gather facts, and think intently about the issue or opportunity. Put a lot of energy and hard work into the task.

2. When you stop feeling productive and begin feeling stressed, walk away from the problem and do something completely different that produces a relaxation response. Take time to do stretches, go for a walk, visit an art museum, listen to soothing music, play with the dog, or enjoy an afternoon tea break. Focus on your breath and calm your mind. This stage of calm and relaxation is the foundation for new insights. When you calm your mind, you can improve focus and productivity.

3. You reach Step 3 when you have an ah-ha experience or get into the zone or optimal flow of thinking. You can get back into the task and your thinking is both smooth and energetic. Answers flow and you are able to focus on the essence of what needs to occur to be successful.

4. Build on this renewed mental clarity and energy. You can use this to impact the rest of your day and week. When you take time to relax your mind and then focus like a laser beam on an important task, the positive mental and physiological response benefits all aspects of your work.

Benson stresses that his four-step breakout technique acknowledges the body's biochemical responses to stress. When exposed to prolonged stress, the body becomes flooded with cortisol, epinephrine, and norepinephrine. When you relax and calm your mind, your body releases nitric oxide, which makes you feel and think better. By practicing these four steps, you can learn to shift your internal biological responses to improve creativity, clarity, and focus.

Let Your Computer Help You Stretch

Arthur Saltzman, inventor and president of Para Technologies, was feeling the stress and strain of prolonged computer use. He felt he needed to be reminded to stretch, so he set up his computer so "Have you stretched recently?" would show up occasionally as he shifted from one program to another. But that wasn't adequate. "I needed something that will really get my attention every half hour or so. And it would be helpful if it showed me some recommended stretches."

To meet his needs, Saltzman created Stretch Break, a computer program that reminds users to stretch and guides them through up to thirty-six different stretches that reduce stress and injuries. To create the product, he formed a panel of health care professionals to select and design stretches. Users can choose the stretches they want to do and how often they want to stretch. Companies such as

Harvard University, 3M, Boeing, Bank of America, and Los Alamos National Labs use Stretch Break to help employees reduce stress and strain. If you could use a reminder to stretch, give Stretch Break a try! More information is available on Saltzman's Web site, www.paratec.com.

True Story

Here is a true story of the benefits of yoga and meditation from a leader we will call Dave.

I have been practicing yoga and meditation for two years. I came to yoga and meditation as a way to find balance in my life, relieve stress, and to relax. I was under a lot of pressure at work. I am the CFO of a financial services business.

While my company provided exceptional and attentive care to its clients, behind the scenes it operated in a vortex of brutal chaos. I now see our overall mode of operation was Darwinian—only the fittest survived. I was given little, if any, direction or communication as a context for clarifying needed actions. I lacked focus and I wasted energy by falling back on old skills. I ran faster, jumped higher, and did more. I found myself spending eighty- and ninety-hour weeks doing unsatisfying work.

I am a husband and father of three children. I love and enjoy my family, but I spent very little time with them. I rarely spent time with myself and was booked from sunup to sundown.

The workload, feelings of failure, and not being able to have time for my family or myself took a heavy toll. Two years ago I almost gave up. I did not think things would improve. Luckily, I decided I would defy insanity (defined as continuing to do the same things and expecting a different result) and try to make workable changes that did not involve moving faster, jumping higher, or doing more.

On my wife's urging I decided to try yoga. She had practiced for a few years and thought it would help me. Up till that point I had resisted and did not expect to like it. I gave it a try and hoped it would offer a combination of relaxation and exercise. I remember well my first session in February 2004. The heat and the confounding poses nearly killed me! What kind of person could do these contortions? I have always been athletic, but have never sweat so much. But I loved it. I felt better. I relaxed. I committed to two days a week and ended up doing three days a week. I rarely missed a session.

I also wanted to establish a meditation practice but found my time too fractured, my body and mind too tired, and little room in my day to spare. I struggled with this for a few months and was nearly to the point of abandoning my goal when I committed to using the early morning from 5:30 A.M. to 7:30 A.M. to meditate. I had been using this time to work at home. Meditating at this time was exactly what I needed.

My yoga practice has taught me a lot that extends to the rest of my life. I focus with total concentration on the poses and don't let thoughts about the day's activities distract me. I have found the following yoga concepts useful outside the yoga studio:

- Do what you can. Drop the judgments, which mask exceptional skills lying below the surface. Let things happen.

- Your body will tell you many things about what is on your mind. Paying attention to your body can help understand what is on your mind and how to take better actions. Paying attention to breathing is very powerful.

- Yoga is not about competition. Worry about your actions, not what others are doing.

- Work on one thing at a time. If you are doing the eagle pose, become one with it. I once was in a pose when a business difficulty from earlier in the day suddenly and mysteriously invaded my thoughts—and I fell over.

- Give up the fruits and focus on the actions. This is karma yoga. It is powerful. When I let go of expectations, sometimes what happens is beyond my wildest dreams.

Meditation has taught me that my mind runs endlessly and restlessly. Tracks that play over and over. I now recognize that thoughts and reality may be very different things. If you can be still and let your mind settle down, you will be granted some space. That space will give you a chance to slow down enough to see more clearly. With that clarity you will find things having different possibilities, you become response-able instead of reactive. The *Tao Te Ching* said, "We shape clay into a pot, but it is the emptiness inside that holds whatever we want. We hammer wood for a house, but it is the inner space that makes it livable. We work with being, but non-being is what we use." Space is a great tool, but all too often we choose busy-ness instead, and we become too full to take coherent action.

I have made great strides in two years. I am more relaxed, focused, and effective at work and home. Could I do more? Yes, but I am pursing my actions and recognizing that the fruits will fall where they may. I can only control how I respond to things. What a great find. *Namaste*.

Part Two

TUNE YOUR DIALOGUE

Coherence is the most interesting property of laser light. This property states that all photons emitted from a laser are at the exact same phase—as waves they all crest and valley at the same time. This property is brought about by the mechanism of the laser itself (stimulated emission) in which photons are essentially copied. In order to stay in phase it is required that all emitted photons are at the exact same wavelength (or very, very close).

—Mark Csele

White light contains many colors of light, each color having its own wavelength. Think of many bouncing balls in a box—or of a flashlight like the one shown in Figure 1. To produce colored light, all the wavelengths but one are filtered out, as pictured in Figure 2. You can produce a red beam of light in this fashion, but that does not give you laser light. Lasers are different because all their photons

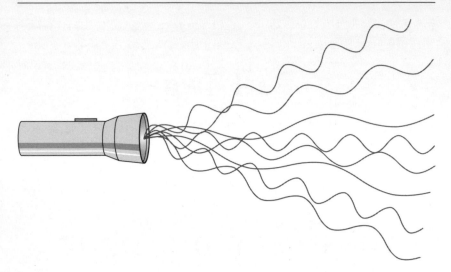

Figure 1

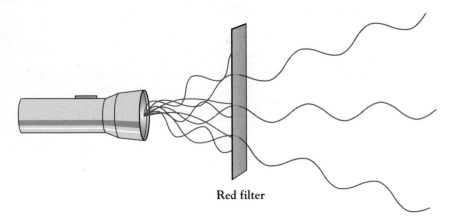

Red filter

Figure 2

Figure 3

are of precisely the same color and therefore wavelength. In addition, the waves are parallel to one another, meaning the crests and troughs of each wave occur in phase, or in step, with one another as shown in Figure 3. This is known as coherence.

Laser-focused leaders know the value of being on the same wavelength with other leaders and employees. Tuned dialogue allows leaders to harness the diverse ideas within the organization while ensuring that messages and conversations are on topic and serving the company goals. Tuned dialogue is a new way of talking at work. It amplifies and crystallizes goals and ideas. In a laser beam, the light is monochromatic. Red beams contain light waves that have only one wavelength and are perfectly in phase. Many particles buzzing to the same drumbeat. The drumbeat of the organization is often determined by its talk. Conversations create the reality of the day and shape the work that is done. Laser-focused leaders use tuned dialogue to create a consistent drumbeat while encouraging diverse ideas, perspectives, and approaches.

Tuned dialogue differs from the usual workplace banter in many ways. It is unlike general conversation because it taps into each individual and elevates your group's thinking. This section shows you how to revolutionize the things about which you and your employees are talking. Talk is the most powerful tool leaders have for creating results. Here are the main characteristics of tuned dialogue:

- *On topic and on point:* The conversation remains focused on the desired outcomes of the conversation.
- *Healthy inquiry and challenge:* Participants ask great questions, hard-hitting questions, and ensure that even tough topics are explored.
- *Connectedness:* Participants feel a sense of shared purpose or interest.
- *Playfulness in a deadly serious way:* The conversation remains businesslike but is also full of energy and interest.
- *Empowerment:* Participants know they can have some impact or influence.

- *Receptivity:* Both speaking and listening occur.
- *Freedom:* Participants feel free to be open and speak candidly.
- *Just-in-time:* Conversations occur when and where needed and are not bound by structured meeting schedules.

Dialogue is the lifeblood of the organization. Leadership is a social act. Imagine catalyzing conversations such that they are stimulating, creative, satisfying, and successful. It is not crazy to envision meetings so productive that nobody dares be late and ad hoc hallway conversations that change the course of business for the better in a breakthrough moment.

5

TURN MEETINGS INTO FOCUS SESSIONS

Creativity does not happen inside people's heads, but in the interaction between a person's thoughts and a sociocultural context.

—Mihaly Csikszentmihalyi

In a Nutshell

Many leaders complain that meetings take up too much of their schedule and are not worth the time and resources spent. The dialogue at many regular update meetings bears them out: it is lethargic and uninspiring. When participants are passive and the topic is not relevant, meetings are a waste of time. Leaders should find better ways to keep employees up to date about what is happening within the company, and then they can transform ineffective meetings into focus sessions.

Better dialogue leads to better results. Focus sessions are a great use of time and attention that will help you tune dialogue. Inquiry that is provocative and evocative engages and stimulates the group's thinking. Focus sessions address one topic, problem, or opportunity, and then go deep into this topic. To achieve laser focus, you need to go deep fast and invite and explore diverse thoughts within the topic.

To ensure focus sessions are successful, invite the right people. Then share the topic, your desired outcomes, and several discussion starting questions before the meeting. When you plan well, the focus and thinking will begin well before your focus session starts.

Meetings top the list of unworthy distractions for many leaders. Too many meetings. Meetings that drag on. Poor meetings. Meetings that most everyone dreads attending and mentally checks out of once crossing the meeting room threshold. Even the best of meetings rarely measure up to what you could be doing with your time. Small e-mail devices, like the BlackBerry, are viewed as saviors. By holding one of these tiny tools just below the tabletop, you can complete other tasks while attending useless meetings. Has it come to this, that the solution is to do *other* work while in meetings? What about focus? What about results? What about being engaged?

The sad truth is that most meetings are not worth the time and salary they devour. The average two-hour staff meeting with eight managers will cost over $1,000 in salaries and benefits. Never mind the opportunity costs of what that time could have been used to accomplish. There is also a residual cost caused by the brain rot induced by many meetings. Does this sound familiar? One or two people control the conversation while most sit biting their tongues to ensure the meeting ends as quickly as possible. The trouble with many meetings is that they allow participants to remain passive.

Related to the problem of passivity is the question of relevance. Many meetings are a waste of time and resources because the topics discussed are unimportant or off-target. How tuned is your litmus test for meeting relevance? If everyone is talking about the items on their to-do lists, is this relevant? In the broadest sense, you could make a case that it is relevant for leaders to share what's on their to-do lists. Relevance depends on how you define the purpose of the meeting. Why are these leaders getting together for two hours? What if you changed the purpose so leaders get together to help collaborate on the company's *most important* problems and opportunities? Would reading to-do lists be relevant then? No, not even close! Meetings can become much more than expensive mechanisms to stay current about what your peers are doing.

You might need to redefine your criteria for what warrants a meeting. To obtain laser focus, all meetings should come with expectations of great dialogue and collaborative conversations. Attending a meeting to hear a one-way conversation is not good enough. Let technology provide methods to convey these messages. Leaders are too busy and their time is too valuable for passive sitting. When you focus like a laser beam, you insist that meetings make a difference and move work forward. Think about what often happens when the manager cancels a staff meeting. People cheer and the work does not suffer. What should this tell leaders? This is a sign that these meetings are more likely barriers than enabling events. When tuned dialogue does not occur, business suffers. The new definition of *meeting relevance:* Dialogue that improves forward movement on an important business priority.

> *Key Point:* Passivity and lack of topic relevance often render meetings useless.

Many meetings contribute to wasted resources and a lack of focus, but none more than ineffective recurring meetings. By their nature, recurring meetings do not encourage new thinking or lively engagement. Such meetings can take up a significant portion of a leader's weekly schedule. This is time that should only be invested in ways that will best contribute to the company's success. Most team meetings, staff meetings, and general update meetings won't meet this hurdle. While it is important that peers stay connected and in communication, the update meeting is often not a good use of time. Find other ways to keep people updated (see this chapter's "In the Real World" section for an example) and use the time in a more valuable kind of meeting: a *focus session*.

> *Key Point:* Recurring meetings are, by their nature, draining and ineffective. Update meetings should be eliminated or simplified.

Characteristics of a Focus Session

The better your dialogue, the better your team will think. The better they think, the better they will act. Better action leads to better results. Better dialogue leads to results. Unfortunately, the reverse is also true. Teams that don't talk about the right stuff won't generate adequate options and input. Without good information, action suffers. Poor action leads to poor results. Poor dialogue harms results.

Great dialogue is the cornerstone of focus sessions. A focus session is a meeting that facilitates progress. Most meetings do not further projects and tasks; instead, they report about the work. Focus sessions facilitate improved momentum and goal clarity and could serve several purposes: help the team get unstuck, generate new ideas, solve a problem, define a cross-functional implementation plan, or take care of some other collective action. The tuned dialogue helps crisp up goals and improves everyone's connection to what needs to be done to produce success.

> *Key Point:* Focus sessions have a dynamic purpose worth people's time and attention.

Focus session dialogue is stimulating and interesting. As a participant, you will find it difficult to remain passive because you will be pulled in by the inquiry. Inquiry is at the core of tuned dialogue. Asking questions is a great way to jump-start dialogue. One question can change the meeting's direction and transform a lackluster conversation into a lively business discussion. As a leader interested in focus, you can be a catalyst within your organization. You have the power and ability to raise the level of tuned dialogue and improve results. The right question could benefit the organization enough to cover your yearly salary or more. Imagine if you facilitated such an inquiry every week. Oh, the difference you would make!

Questions come in several types, and they are far from equal. The two most common types of questions are closed and open-ended.

- *Closed questions:* Ask for a short or one-word answer. (Do you want to be successful?)
- *Open-ended questions:* Ask for a longer, individualized answer. (What would you like to accomplish this year?)

To create effective inquiry, you need to look deeper than whether the question is open-ended or closed. Both types can be poor or excellent questions, although open-ended elicit more comprehensive answers. The two examples I just listed are both poor questions. They are uninteresting and overly general. By contrast, another way to look at creating inquiry focuses on the *quality* of the questions you ask. As a leader, you want to make sure that your questions are provocative or evocative.

- *Provocative questions:* Excite and stimulate conversation. (What would happen if . . . ?)

- *Evocative questions:* Pull in participants and help bring things to mind. (What kind of work makes you feel most engaged and satisfied?)

You want to select questions that move the topic forward and engage the group. When creating inquiry, the more questions you ask, the better. But they need to be great questions. If you are the type of person who is comfortable sharing your opinions and ideas, your challenge will be to resist giving advice. Advice rarely improves inquiry.

> *Key Point:* Focus sessions are both provocative and evocative. They spark inquiry and inspire participants to improve connectivity and engagement.

Focus sessions address one topic, one problem, one aspect of one problem, or even one possible way to address one aspect of one problem. The key number is *one*. The problem with many meetings is that participants end up discussing many topics and none in enough depth to make much difference. To focus like a laser beam, you want dialogue that is an inch wide and mile deep. In other words, you should promote conversations that delve deep into a single problem or opportunity.

Within one topic of discussion, you should seek diverse ideas and perspectives. Explore the topic in various contexts and look at the issue from several angles. Embrace open discussion, even if this causes dissonance. If this task or project is one in which the company has struggled, invite an open conversation about why failure occurred. As David Perkins wrote in *Archimedes' Bathtub* (2000), "There's being wrong or insightfully wrong." At the focus session, help participants go deep into the topic quickly by asking questions that will fuel passionate dialogue.

> *Key Point:* Focus sessions go an inch wide and mile deep.
> Topics are clear and the conversation goes deep fast.

Don't make it difficult for people to participate in effective dialogue. When scheduling a focus session, you need to define the topic of the meeting and give participants time to prepare. Let them know your desired outcome and share some of your best questions (*best* meaning most provocative or evocative, the questions that will stimulate conversation). If you share questions before the meeting, you will find that thinking, dialogue, and focus will begin right away. When the focus session starts, participants will be ready to engage and go deep into the topic. When you invite people to the meeting, encourage them to bring sources of information.

Who should you invite to your focus session? You will want to have a smallish group of individuals (no more than fifteen) who can each add to the topic. Be sure to invite both supporters of your ideas and probable or known opponents. It is important to have a diversity of perspectives and opinions. Don't let hierarchy or politics determine who attends your focus session. A group made up of a couple of managers from different functions, a few frontline workers, an analyst, and the resident critic might offer you better dialogue and results than a team of people at the same level or in the same function.

> *Key Point:* Focus, attention, and thinking begin before the
> focus session starts. Be sure you prepare attendees for optimal
> participation and invite people who can add to the topic.

Focus sessions are a great antidote to today's meeting crisis. Too many meetings. Ineffective meetings. Meetings that people dread. Stop the craziness now. Use the time you spend with your coworkers to further the work and improve focus.

In the Real World

Are you ready to schedule a focus session? Here is a meeting worksheet, sample questions, and story that can help you get started. Try replacing half of your staff meetings with focus sessions for two months. Search for new ways to provide information updates and slowly reduce the number of recurring meetings you schedule. Use huddles (introduced in Chapter Seven) to do quick updates and ensure people are clear about priorities.

Focus Session Worksheet

This worksheet will help you plan, communicate, and conduct a focus session.

Focus Session Planning Worksheet
Topic: Note: Be sure you focus on one task, problem, opportunity, or a portion of one of these. Can you create excellent dialogue around this one topic in the time you have available?
Desired Outcomes: What do you want to accomplish by end of this meeting? 1. 2.
Inquiry: List five provocative or evocative questions that will promote engagement and focused dialogue. 1. 2. 3. 4. 5.

Participants: Who can best contribute to this topic?	
1.	6.
2.	7.
3.	8.
4.	9.
5.	10.

Invite: Send invitations to the participants and share the topic, desired outcomes, and the five questions you detailed above. Allow at least forty-eight hours of preparation time if possible.
Prep: Set up the meeting room in advance and post or hand out the topic, desired outcomes, and questions. If you need to participate in the discussion, consider asking a trainer or peer to run the meeting for you.
During the meeting: Periodically check to ensure the conversation is on topic. Remind participants about the desired outcomes if necessary. Manage overparticipators and ensure everyone is heard. Encourage and appreciate opposing views. Address what's *not* being said. Take good notes. Offer refreshments if meeting is longer than ninety minutes.
After the meeting: Thank participants for their input and act on the information they provided you. Responsiveness is the best thanks. Communicate changes or progress to ensure everyone is clear (use a huddle, e-mail, internal blog, MBWA, or other communication vehicle).

You will notice that the worksheet asks you to list the topic, desired outcome, and questions before defining participants. This is important. If you define the participants before you determine the questions you will ask, it is more likely that you will not have the right people present to create effective tuned dialogue.

Sample Provocative Questions

Provocative questions are exciting, stimulating, or intellectually interesting. Here are several generic provocative questions you can tweak to fit your topic. Use liberally as needed!

- We have seen more close calls in operations. Are you comfortable with the procedures we have in place to prevent accidents? If not, why not?

- I sent each of you the time line and milestones for the upgrade project yesterday. What have we missed? Can we implement this change fully and well? If not, why not? What will things look like in a year if everything goes as planned?

- Today's discussion is focused on how to improve output to the [name a specific] process. It has been suggested that we eliminate [one particular step]. What impact will removing this step have on the rest of the process?

- How would our customers want us to do this? How do our competitors do this? Given our mission, how should we differentiate ourselves from the competition?

- Share an idea that you think would work but would never be considered. What's the wildest idea you can think of?

- What would a home run look like?

- What's getting in the way? Why do these barriers exist? How do we get rid of these barriers?

- What trends or emerging changes should we be aware of and consider?

- Is this project more important than [name another project]?

What should we stop doing or change to enable more time and focus for this project?

- How do we put this together into a clear and focused action plan?

Sample Evocative Questions

Evocative questions facilitate reflection and have people see themselves in the situation. They call people forward or pull them into a situation or topic. Here are several generic evocative questions you can tweak to fit your topic. Use these to create greater connection and relationship to the topic.

- If you could change one thing about this process, what would you change?
- How would you like the change to occur?
- How does this help you achieve your goal? What does this mean to you?
- What generalizations or assumptions have you made? How do you know that [some specific thing behaves as it does]? Have you seen a situation similar to this before?
- What are the pros and cons of your idea? How is this similar to or different from the way you have approached this in the past?
- How do you define success relative to this project?
- If this change were implemented, what corresponding changes would you recommend for your team?
- What do you worry about most? What keeps you up at night?
- How would you like to define your role in this project?
- If you were in my position, how would you do this differently?

True Story

Cruise West is a niche cruise line catering to retired and semiretired customers who want to get up close to nature and cultures. A group of about six met to discuss the next brochure for the Sea of Cortés and Baja California itinerary. These marketing project meetings happened fairly often, and generally went something like this:

- Each participant reviewed the prior year's brochure before the meeting and made notes about changes needed in the new brochure. Changes included port calls, shore excursions, entertainment, celebrations, logistics, and the general flow of the trip.
- During the meeting, the members each shared their suggestions for what needed to be changed. The group discussed these suggestions and agreed on how much would change in each aspect of the tour.
- The group discussed deadlines for creative content, layout, when files would go to the printers, and when the brochures would be ready to distribute.

These project meetings served to clarify what needed to change in the next edition of the brochure. This particular marketing project meeting, however, took an unexpected turn. When the director of product development, the person in charge of creating the trips, was asked what needed to change, her response set the meeting on end. She said that while few details about the trip were changing for the next year, she did not think the brochure shared the compelling aspects of the trip. She said that she knew what made the experience amazing, but failed to see this come through in the copy and pictures that made up the brochure. The day-by-day review was accurate, the list of ports was correct, and the shore excursions were listed properly. What was missing was why people should visit this special region of the world with Cruise West.

At first, the meeting participants were a bit quiet, but then the conversation took off. The meeting transformed into a focus session. They began asking great questions and together they explored their assumptions and goals for the brochure. The dialogue became interesting and lively and by the end of the meeting, all participants felt more connected and interested in telling the story of the Sea of Cortés trip. In their minds, the gorgeous and dramatic geology stood large and strong. Schools of dolphins jumped with the rhythm of the ship. Centuries-old cultures passed along their charm, generosity, and wisdom. They felt the bumpy softness of the blue whale's nose as it rose to greet their ponga boat. They screeched underwater in joy as young sea lions performed water ballet around them so close they could feel the animals playfully brush past. The region came to life in their talk, then in their minds, and ultimately in the next brochure. This team experienced laser focus because the dialogue was able to escape the everyday patterns and become lively, engaging, and interesting. The brochure was completely redesigned and the time line had to be tossed out and redefined. But the delay and their focused work paid off.

An Alternative to Update Meetings

It's easy to ensure everyone has the information they need without sitting them down in a group and pouring it onto their heads. Many companies are turning to internal blogs to help fill the need for good and dynamic communication. An internal blog is a Web log, or an online journal that is used by employees. Here are the benefits of internal blogs:

- Information can be posted and updated quickly.
- An active blog is like conversation. Employees can leave comments, clarifications, and questions. Other employees can respond to comments and answer questions.
- Pictures, graphs, and charts can easily be added to reinforce the information.
- Posts can be categorized and searched.
- Blogging can be an entertaining and engaging way to communicate well.

If you use an internal blog, recommend that employees make the blog the home page of their Internet browser. You will also need to create a basic policy that defines the rules for posting and commenting. You can find sample policies by searching the Internet. A small call center decided to use an internal blog as its central source for information and created links on the left and right columns to their product information and policies. Readership among sales agents was high because the blog contained the information they needed and was fun to boot!

True Story

This blog post (from "Leadership Now") summarizes how one leader chose to replace regular staff meetings.

Beyond Staff Meetings
by Don Blohowiak

Not everyone likes regular staff meetings. They can get stale. Feel like make-work. Waste time.

When he was a prosecutor in Maryland, Bob Coyne, who now consults with courts and corporations on management and leadership matters, was a boss who rejected the routine staff meeting.

"I just hate them," he says. So instead of forcing very busy people to sit passively for a lot of blah-blah-blah, Coyne kept people apprised of current developments by communicating through other means. And, significantly, he would invite meaningful feedback by occasionally asking his staff two questions.

1. If you had my authority in the organization, what changes would you make right now?

2. What am I doing that gets in the way of you doing your best work here?

"These two questions give you great information," Coyne says.

Whether you hold regular staff meetings or not, putting these two questions to your colleagues could yield a wealth of insights—without a bunch of blah-blah-blah.

6

INVITE A CHALLENGE

The strongest oak tree of the forest is not the one that is protected
from the storm and hidden from the sun. It's the one that stands in
the open where it is compelled to struggle for its existence against the
winds and rains and the scorching sun.

—Napoleon Hill

In a Nutshell

Challenges bring out the best in people and enable them to focus. The best
leaders thrive on challenges and are open to learning from people at all levels within the organization. It is difficult to focus without healthy challenges.
Laser-focused leaders push beyond their emotional discomfort to encourage
candid, future-oriented feedback and diverse ideas. Adopt a "Bring it on!" at-
titude today to improve your focus, satisfaction, and results.

You can invite a challenge in several ways. Hire only the best and brightest people, those who can challenge you and their fellow team members. You
should also encourage saves—that is, feedback that helps prevent problems.
If you want to know what's not working, you need to value and reinforce
timely saves. Another way to invite a challenge is to ask peers and team
members to shoot holes in your ideas and plans; this is feedback focused on
the future. Do this as your plans are coming together so you have time to adjust and strengthen them. Try Marshall Goldsmith's feedforward technique.

The best way to ensure that you get helpful input is to ask for it. Ask interesting questions and reinforce those who offer feedback with your thanks
and by using their input to improve the work.

Friedrich Nietzsche, the German philosopher and social critic, was a little more blunt than Napoleon Hill: "What does not destroy me, makes me stronger." Regardless of whether you prefer your aphorisms strong and black or mixed with cream and sugar, it is an inescapable fact that challenges bring out the best in people.

In 2003, LPGA (Ladies Professional Golf Association) tour pro Annika Sorenstam played the men of the PGA (Professional Golf Association) tour in the Colonial Tournament. With nerves high and in front of huge crowds, she played well but missed the cut by four shots. When asked why she wanted to compete against the men, Sorenstam replied that she mainly wanted to see what she could do and reenergize her game. "I'm not putting the guys on test here, or men against women. I'm far from that," she said. "This is a test for me personally. I don't want to put the guys on any defensive. I just want to play against the best and see what happens." The following season, she played eighteen LPGA tournaments, winning eight and finishing in the top ten in sixteen of them.

Look closely and you will see this theme repeating itself in many aspects of life. Weekend warriors head to the squash court and give the game their all. They want to play against great players who will challenge them, not beginners they could beat with ease. Even when they lose, if the game is close, it means they fought hard and played their best. Young actors gush with pride and healthy intimidation when they get to work with the greats like Robert de Niro and Meryl Streep. What they learn watching these veterans in action rivals a lifetime's worth of lessons in acting school. The best scientists and engineers thrive on challenges. They recruit the most promising graduate students and brightest colleagues for their research labs, and feel compelled to take on difficult problems rather than easy ones. Weekend squash players, actors, or high-tech geniuses—they all know that working with the best raises their game to a new level.

An ancient Chinese proverb says people seek a challenge just as fire seeks to flame. Challenge is exciting and nourishing; your brain's synapses fire as you generate new and interesting thoughts. A challenge is a demanding or stimulating experience. To challenge something can mean to question it or offer a contest. A challenge calls for you to step up and be your best. Leaders grow and improve their abilities when they seek out challenges. It is impossible to focus if you do not know how well your decisions and actions match up to your potential. Are you doing your best? Could you be trying harder? To be at your best and focus like a laser, you need to be open and receptive to ideas, concerns, and feedback. All leaders need to be challenged.

Great leaders seek out the company and opinions of talented people. They thrive when surrounded by bright, creative, and caring peers and managers. These leaders even go so far as hiring gifted people from whom they might learn. Soichiro Honda, namesake of the automobile company, agrees that inviting a challenge is critical. "If you hire only those people you understand, the company will never get people better than you are. Always remember that you often find outstanding people among those you don't particularly like." Honda's thoughts put a slightly different twist on the notion of inviting a challenge; the best people not only challenge us in ways that raise our game, they might also be people that we simply don't like. Laser-focused leaders want to be around greatness, and they do not feel threatened by the accomplishments of others. In fact, acknowledging the success of others is both therapeutic and uplifting.

Key Point: Being open to learning from others helps leaders focus and excel.

Inviting a challenge can save your hide. If you establish an environment where people feel comfortable sharing their concerns and questioning actions and decisions, you are more likely to catch mistakes and head off problems before something truly bad happens. If you come across as defensive in meetings or demonstrate that you do not want to be made to look wrong, you will not benefit from helpful information that others could share. Your peers, managers, and team members are in a position to see problems as they emerge. You want to know what's happening as soon as possible; otherwise your options for dealing with issues will quickly diminish.

Inviting a challenge can be a wonderful and enjoyable experience when leaders keep their egos from getting in the way. It is human to feel embarrassed when someone finds and communicates a mistake or potential misstep. You may feel inadequate or attacked when challenged in front of a group or during a meeting. If it is important for you to appear in control or look good in front of others, you might find that inviting a challenge is the greatest challenge of all. Regardless of how easy or difficult you find it to invite challenges, you cannot obtain laser focus if you are not engaged in tuned dialogue about important work priorities. If your information is filtered or incomplete, you cannot possibly make the best judgments and your results will suffer. To combat this, redefine success in a way that makes those around you comfortable with and committed to sharing their feedback, concerns, and ideas. When you invite a challenge, you have greater control of your business and your results make you look good.

> *Key Point:* You want to know what's not going well and when things are working.

Bring it on! Take on this mantra for a month and see how it improves your focus and results. Laser-focused leaders invite others to evaluate and take shots at their ideas and plans. They want to know what makes sense and what is unclear. They want to understand where potential barriers might rear their ugly heads. They want to know the parts of the plan that provoke the best and worst responses. They want to hear alternatives that might help strengthen the plan's implementation.

Inviting a challenge to your best-laid plans improves focus in two ways. First, your plans will become stronger and easier to implement. With better information, you can adjust a plan and reduce the barriers to approval and execution. Second, you will have created healthy tuned dialogue that builds support and alignment. When you involve others in conversations about upcoming projects, they have a chance to prepare mentally and begin their transition. In addition, when people have the opportunity to provide input, and when they see that their leader has heard them, their connection and dedication to the project and leader increases.

> *Key Point:* Laser-focused leaders ask peers and team members to shoot holes in their ideas and plans.

Leaders let others know whether they welcome challenges in many ways. In meetings, their nonverbal demeanor tells the group whether they are open to input or would rather not hear concerns or alternative ideas. Do you look down at your agenda or at the wall clock when people speak up? Do you smile and give direct eye contact to people brave enough to challenge your ideas? The types of questions that leaders ask, or the absence of questions, communicates the kinds of responses they seek. Do you defend ideas or ask people to tell you more about their concerns? Is tuned dialogue encouraged during team meetings? When leaders use and respond to input, they communicate they value a challenge. What would your staff say about you? Would they describe you as someone who invites challenges in the spirit of improvement or someone who shuns even the smallest piece of criticism? Make sure that your verbal and nonverbal communication is consistent with your interest in and intent to welcome input.

> *Key Point:* Verbally and nonverbally, leaders communicate whether they are receptive to a challenge.

If you want to invite a challenge, ask for it. Ask for input at meetings. Ask for input during informal conversations. Schedule meetings for the sole purpose of inviting a challenge. When people offer their ideas, ask for more information and seek to understand fully what they are saying. Ask others whether they share the concerns and reinforce those with the courage to bring up tough subjects. Leaders want to be challenged to ensure they are focusing on the most important aspects of the problem and are not wasting time or resources. They will create an environment where they can regularly request and receive candid feedback. If someone challenges you, consider it a gift. Show respect and appreciation, and you will receive more input and more valuable information.

Inviting a challenge is not the same as inviting distraction. Be careful not to use the need for information and analysis to justify inaction or diversions. Ask for a challenge as plans are being conceived and be responsive to any necessary adjustments during implementation. You do not want to waste your time second-guessing plans to the point that you investigate too many options or try to accomplish too many objectives with a single program. Ask for input at the appropriate times to ensure your projects and plans are robust and consider the collective intelligence of your group and peers.

> *Key Point:* The best way to invite a challenge is to ask for a challenge.

Inviting a challenge means using tuned dialogue to improve the quality and flow of information. Leaders who see that alternative views, setbacks, and mistakes are important opportunities for learning and adjustment are better able to obtain and maintain laser focus.

In the Real World

Are you ready to invite a challenge? Here are several ideas for ways you can request valuable input, Marshall Goldsmith's feedforward technique, and a real story of one company that scored big while inviting a challenge. This chapter closes with words of wisdom about making mistakes from legendary communicator Dale Carnegie.

How to Invite a Challenge

Communicate both verbally and nonverbally that you are open to input, and use methods that produce regular and effective feedback. Find the solutions that fit best with your style and your company. Here are several ideas:

• *Create super users:* Harnessing the knowledge of super users doesn't just apply to computer systems, although this is where they're used the most. You can apply the super user concept to many disciplines. Create a group of topical experts and go to them again and again for feedback. Super users are also trusted with the authority to modify files and administer the system in ways that regular users are not. Do you place that kind of trust in your employees? Show your super users that you value their expertise and make them feel special. They are special!

• *Pilot projects:* Conduct small-scale runs on plans and projects before launching them throughout the company. The purpose of a pilot project is to test what works and to learn where adjustments are needed. When you do this, you need to actively seek input and remain accessible to those involved.

• *Extreme feedback sessions (also known as Focus Sessions, as in Chapter Five):* If you are working on an important project or plan, you may want to schedule a focus session. Ask participants to take shots at your rough draft and share their ideas and concerns. The meeting should be long enough to allow everyone to share their feedback and for you to ask clarifying questions.

• *Surround yourself with greatness:* Hire people who will challenge you, not bow to you. This is especially important in industries where high levels of technical expertise are required. You cannot be an expert in everything, but you can hire people who collectively cover all the fields you need. Actively participate in professional organizations that attract the best and brightest in your field. Attend local and national professional meetings or, better yet, volunteer to speak at those meetings. Seek assignments both on and off the job that allow you to work side by side with leaders whom you admire.

- *Go public with ideas:* It is difficult to invite a challenge if others do not know your goals or ideas. Share your thoughts in rough form and as they become more developed. Use internal and external blogs to test and refine ideas. Enjoy lunch with a peer and ask your companion for a reaction to your idea.

- *Involve your best customers:* Loyal customers know your products and services best. Many companies ask customers to be guinea pigs for new ideas. Software publishers use alpha and beta testers, many of whom are loyal customers, to put new versions to the test and evaluate new features. Likewise, high-end outdoor gear manufacturers rely on professional mountaineers to test new designs and materials. In exchange, the companies get wonderful feedback and the customers build a connection to the company. You can apply this idea internally as well. Who are your internal customers? Why not ask them for feedback?

- *Encourage curiosity:* Work environments should foster focused curiosity. Leaders can encourage curiosity by asking great questions, responding favorably to intellectual exploration, and being inquisitive. Allow time in meetings to discuss ideas and ask provocative and evocative questions. Some companies actively encourage employees to pursue new ideas on company time. One of the best-known examples of this is Google, where employees are free to pursue their own ideas for up to 20 percent of their work time. Three of the top suggestions emerging from this program are Google News, Google Answers (a pay-by-the-question service), and the Google desktop bar that allows users to search without opening a Web browser.

As Albert Einstein wrote, "The important thing is not to stop questioning. Curiosity has its own reason for existing. One cannot help but be in awe when he contemplates the mysteries of eternity, of life, of the marvelous structure of reality. It is enough if one tries merely to comprehend a little of this mystery every day. Never lose a holy curiosity."

- *Reward saves:* A *save* is an action taken by someone that prevents something undesirable from happening. In baseball, saves are valued and tracked. How much difference can a save make? Bobby Thigpen, a relief pitcher for the Chicago White Sox, set a major league record by saving fifty-seven games for his team in 1990. That's almost exactly one-third of the games played in a major league baseball season. In the NFL (National Football League), players who make interceptions can change the direction and momentum of the game. How well do you acknowledge and appreciate people who make saves at work? Make sure your team members and peers know that you seek and welcome saves.

Try Feedforward

Marshall Goldsmith is an executive coach and the founding director of the Alliance for Strategic Leadership. He recommends leaders ask for ideas focused on the future, not feedback about the past, a technique he calls *feedforward:*

> In addition to giving feedback, start giving feedforward—focus on the promise of the future rather than the mistakes of the past. Giving and receiving feedback has long been considered an essential skill for leaders. People need to know how they are doing, whether or not their performance meets expectations, and how to improve. Traditionally, this information has been communicated in the form of feedback from leaders, who need feedback in the form of suggestions for improvement, innovative ideas for new products and services, and input on their leadership styles. This information is commonly given in 360-degree feedback, but such feedback focuses on past events—not on the infinite possibilities of the future. Feedback is limited and static, as opposed to expansive and dynamic.
>
> I have observed more than 5,000 leaders as they play two roles. In one, they are asked to provide feedforward—to give someone else suggestions for the future and help as much as they can. In the second role, they are asked to accept feedforward—to listen to suggestions for the future and learn as much as they can. They are not allowed to give feedback about the past.

In this feedforward exercise, people are asked to:

- Choose to change one behavior to make a positive difference in their lives.

- Describe this behavior to others.

- Ask for two suggestions for achieving a positive change in the behavior.

- Listen to suggestions and take notes without commenting on them.

- Thank others for their suggestions.

- Ask others what they would like to change.

- Provide feedforward—two suggestions aimed at helping them change.

- Say, "You are welcome," when thanked for the suggestions.

Giving and receiving feedforward only takes about two minutes. When asked to describe this experience, people use words like "great, energizing, useful, helpful, fun." Few of us think of feedback as fun!"

Marshall Goldsmith offers the following ten reasons to try feedforward:

1. We can change the future, not the past. Feedforward helps people envision and focus on a positive future, not a failed past. By giving people ideas on how they can be even more successful, we increase their chances of success.

2. It is more productive to help people be right, than prove them wrong. Negative feedback often becomes an exercise in proving others wrong. This tends to produce defensiveness on the part of the receiver and discomfort on the part of the sender. Even constructive feedback is often seen as negative. Feedforward is positive. It focuses on solutions.

3. Successful people like getting ideas aimed at helping them achieve their goals. They tend to resist negative judgment, accepting feedback that is consistent with the way they see

themselves and rejecting or denying other feedback. They respond to (and even enjoy) feedforward.

4. Feedforward can come from anyone who knows the task, not just the person. Almost any one can give you ideas on how you can improve. They don't have to know you. Feedback requires knowing the person. Feedforward just requires having helpful ideas.

5. People do not take feedforward as personally as feedback. Constructive feedback is supposed to focus on the performance, not the person, and yet most feedback is taken personally.

6. Feedforward assumes that people can make positive changes in the future, whereas feedback tends to reinforce stereotyping, self-fulfilling prophecies, and feelings of failure. How many of us have been "helped" by a spouse, friend, or colleague who recites our "sins" and shortcomings? Negative feedback reinforces the message, "This is just the way you are."

7. Most of us hate getting negative feedback, and we don't like to give it. Most of us are not very good at giving or receiving negative feedback. Nor do we value the more positive skills of "providing timely feedback" and "encouraging and accepting constructive criticism."

8. Feedforward can cover most of the same "material" as feedback, but in a more positive manner. Imagine that you just made a terrible presentation. Using the feedforward approach, your manager helps you prepare for future presentations by giving you very specific suggestions in a positive way, rather than make you "relive" this humiliating experience.

9. Feedforward tends to be more efficient and effective than feedback. For example, in giving ideas to people, you might say, "Here are four ideas for the future. Please accept them in the positive spirit that they are given. If you can only use two of the ideas, you are still ahead. Just ignore what doesn't make sense for you." With this approach, no time is wasted on judging the ideas or proving them wrong.

10. Feedforward can be used with managers, peers, and team members. Rightly or wrongly, feedback is associated with judgment. This can lead to very negative outcomes. Feedforward does not imply superior judgment. Since it is more focused on being helpful, it is easier to hear. Invite people to ask, "How can I better help our team in the future?" and listen to feedforward from fellow team members.

A True Story

Marketing guru Seth Godin recently started a new company called Squidoo. Before it went live, he invited people to check out its product and offer feedback. He did this in a way that seemed to make those offering the initial feedback feel privileged and special. He also communicated the company's interest in input in a way that increased conversation and support for the initiative. Here is a quote from the Squidoo blog regarding the beta testers:

> We kicked off Squidoo's closed beta test today, inviting just a few hundred people to help us kick the tires and refine the platform before our public beta launch. It's probably an understatement to say we're excited. These are the first people, outside of our small team, to see what we've been building. It's not perfect, it's not done, but it's ready to try. If you requested a beta invitation and didn't make the first wave, don't worry. We'll be inviting additional testers on a rolling basis as the beta test progresses. And if you haven't requested an invitation yet, it's not too late: Just ask. Even if you don't get in, you'll still be the first to know when we launch.

Why not try something like this inside your organization? Make people feel special for testing your plans and create positive buzz for upcoming changes.

The Importance of Admitting Mistakes

Many leaders feel embarrassed when they make mistakes, and then they allow this emotion to get in the way of their reaction and responses. Fear of being embarrassed keeps some people from inviting a challenge. There is another way to see and respond to mistakes.

Dale Carnegie's *How to Win Friends and Influence People* was originally published in the 1930s. It's a great book about business dialogue and relationships that offers a history lesson on the side. Here's how it approaches mistakes:

> Any fool can try to defend his or her mistakes—and most fools do— but it raises one above the herd and gives one a feeling of nobility and exultation to admit one's mistakes. For example, one of the most beautiful things that history records about Robert E. Lee is the way he blamed himself, and only himself, for the failure of Pickett's charge at Gettysburg.
>
> When we are right, let's try to win people gently and tactfully to our way of thinking, and when we are wrong—and that will be surprisingly often, if we are honest with ourselves—let's admit our mistakes quickly and with enthusiasm. Not only will that technique produce astonishing results; but believe it or not, it is a lot more fun, under the circumstances, than trying to defend oneself [Carnegie, 1990, p. 139].

Robert E. Lee didn't just forget to act on an action item or miss a quarterly sales target. He ordered an attack that turned into a bloodbath for his troops, who suffered a 50 percent casualty rate. Brigadier General Lewis Armistead was mortally wounded as he led the charge on horseback, despite the fact that he knew it would mean certain death. Instead of blaming the disaster on someone else or reflecting upon it in his memoirs, Lee apologized to his troops as they staggered back and tried to regroup in fear of a counterattack.

Energetically admit mistakes immediately. Then open yourself up for tuned dialogue about how to proceed and succeed.

7

HUDDLE

We changed our image. At least when we ran out on the field or broke the huddle, we would look like winners.

—Hayden Fry, quoted in *Coach*, by Carol Harker

In a Nutshell

Huddles are short and lively conversations shared by a small group—anywhere from three to ten team members, peers, or coworkers. They are real-time conversations held in person or over the phone. Huddles are excellent tools for improving clarity and focus without slowing down the work pace. Huddles help participants focus on what needs to be accomplished now and stay calibrated within the team. Huddles can be called any time and by anyone. Leadership changes with the topic. While huddles might technically be called meetings, try not to think of them in this way. Huddles are shorter and more energetic. Don't let your huddles turn into the myriad of dreaded meetings that fill the typical leader's schedule!

You should use huddles to make sure priorities are focused, clear, and agreed to by all team members. You can also use huddles to keep a project flowing well or to deal with emerging issues or opportunities. Huddles are also excellent vehicles for celebrating successes. To give huddles a try, pull your group together each morning for a week and share your top three priorities for the day. Have the group stand in a circle to help make sure the huddle doesn't turn itself into a regular meeting.

◆ ◆ ◆

On brisk fall Monday nights, millions watch the huddle in action. Football team members and coaches huddle before the game. They huddle on the sidelines. Players huddle on the field for less than forty-five seconds but accomplish a lot. Occasionally they skip a huddle to keep up the speed and momentum of the game and to prevent their opponent from benefiting from a huddle. Quick sideline huddles ensure all players are crystal clear about what needs to happen next. The huddle is a primary method of communication in the National Football League. It serves to ensure that each team member is focused like a laser beam on winning each game, quarter, drive, and play.

At TGI Friday's restaurants, huddles are also important. At the beginning of each shift, the wait staff and kitchen staff meet briefly to kick-start the day. Topics include daily specials, 86'd items (dishes that can't be prepared that day), lessons learned from the previous shift, and any special parties or events. Then, as the lunch shift winds down and the dinner shift gets ready to gear up, there are more huddles. The night crew meets, then several smaller huddles occur between outgoing and incoming WWs (what they call waiters and waitresses) and cooks. Shift managers huddle to ensure consistent management and delivery of product.

At Walt Disney World, huddles are an integral part of the company culture and occur on multiple levels. Globally, a daily operational huddle is usually held at the "hub" of the park. Here the daily park duty manager meets with directors of various operating divisions—Attractions, Food Services, Merchandise, Custodial, and Entertainment—to review the day's activities, attendance projections, and weather updates. Department leaders share important information such as operational changes in their respective areas. When the gates of the park open, each area is ready, and leaders can return with a game plan for daily business changes. In addition, huddles are used on a local level by team leaders, coordinators, and managers to report daily operational information to the frontline staff. Each cast member can then anticipate any changes to the show and respond correctly.

The use of huddles in team sports, service establishments, and entertainment theme parks seems logical. Each day, people in these organizations need to get jazzed up to perform for their customers. It is critical that all the players and employees know their roles and how to ensure a win for the day. Each day brings new information on which to act and special considerations that must be widely understood. Are football clubs, restaurants, and playhouses different from the average corporate work environment? Is huddling a practice best suited to sports and hospitality? Not at all. While differences exist in all industries, they all share commonalities that reinforce the potential benefits of using huddles everywhere.

Using a huddle is beneficial for any team that needs to perform and execute daily. This would include most teams working in private and public organizations. Your team can either have a great day or something less. Many factors determine how each day will go and barriers pop up to challenge your planning and resources. To stay connected and current, you need a tool that will keep you and your team plugged in and engaged. Huddles can fulfill these needs and others.

You have heard of MBWA, right? That's management by wandering around, a practice that enables leaders to be accessible and knowledgeable about what's really going on. MBWA is valuable in that it is spontaneous, informal, and responsive. When you use MBWA you can see conditions as they emerge and get to know your team members more fully. Huddling offers some of the same benefits, applied to a small group. The real-time nature of huddles helps groups stay current and responsive. Each huddle focuses on a near-term time frame, such as a week, day, or half-day, and helps team members get on the same page about what they need to do. Huddles also help members understand and prepare for current conditions. Huddles should occur frequently and can be held on a regular or ad hoc basis. A huddle can pick up where the last one left off, or it can deal with a different topic or project.

> *Key Point:* Regular huddles ensure calibration of what needs to happen now.

Huddles can include the whole team or parts of it. Sometimes huddles are regular, like at the beginning of an offensive drive, lunch shift, or workday. Huddles should also be used as situations evolve. For example, you may want to try a huddle the next time your team experiences a barrier. Addressing the situation quickly and informally will help you understand your options for solving the problem. Serious problems will warrant further investigation and perhaps more formal meetings, but a huddle is a great place to start on most everyday situations. Any team member can call a huddle and the leader of the huddle changes with the task. As a team leader you will want to encourage all your people to call huddles when needed and to run the huddle when appropriate.

> *Key Point:* Huddles can be called any time, by any team member, and the leadership changes.

The key differences between a huddle and a meeting are size, focus, and length. The ideal number of people for a huddle is between three and ten. If you have larger teams, consider breaking them into smaller groups based on their shared responsibilities. Many meetings go on for an hour or more while huddles should last ten minutes or less. Many huddles conclude in just a couple of minutes. The best huddles are lightning fast! Huddles deal with one focus, topic, or project, and they improve the pace of work. Long, drawn-out meetings that lack focus slow the work pace and sap team members' energy. Huddling is usually done in an office, within the work environment, or in a meeting room. You might stand for the entire huddle or sit briefly. Encourage team members to hold quick huddles in their workspace, particularly when they are leading the discussion and may have materials or visuals to share.

> *Key Point:* Huddles are quick; don't let huddles become meetings.

Huddles are unique in that they engage the entire group in the conversation. Everyone has a role to play and a contribution to make to the team's success that day. When in a huddle, acknowledge all the members individually and clarify their part in the action. Huddles should not focus on two out of six people or become a one-on-one conversation with several observers. In addition, because leadership of huddles change with the topic, all members take their turn guiding the team and contributing their ideas and recommendations. Here's another benefit of huddles: they help people who usually irritate each other partner productively. Why? The conversation sticks to what's going on and everyone's roles and does not stray into emotionally charged areas. Because huddles are business focused and fast, they enable diverse styles and personalities to work well together. Huddles focus and keep people's attention on the tasks at hand. When you talk about one task, one project, one challenge, one opportunity, there is less room for misinterpretation.

> *Key Point:* Huddles encourage active engagement and connection.

It is best to huddle in person, but in today's global work environment of cross-functional, cross-country teams, huddling over the phone also works. It is important that each member of the huddle is able to contribute in real time. It is the energetic interplay of active conversation that makes huddling a great way to tune dialogue. Can this be done online? Maybe. As work-sharing applications improve, it is possible that quality huddles may be able to occur online. Huddling by e-mail is not recommended because the conversation will not occur in real time and involve all parties. The active nature of a conversation is lost when using e-mail and an e-mail huddle will not offer the same advantages of improving pace and connectedness.

> *Key Point:* You can huddle in person or on the phone, but not by e-mail.

In the Real World

Want to give the huddle a try? Here are several huddles for you to consider and test. Different types of huddles fit each situation or environment. It is not suggested that you implement all these huddles—your people would feel huddled out. Huddles should be nonintrusive—a quick check-in to ensure understanding, support, and focus. Share these examples, including the sample dialogue and questions, with your team members before trying the huddle for the first time.

The Individual Excellence Huddle

For the next five days, huddle with your team near the start of each shift. The huddle should last no more than five minutes. Each member of the team will come to the huddle with a 3×5 card listing three top priorities for the day to read to the group. As each card is read, other team members will ask clarifying questions and agree or disagree that these should be on the top of the reader's list. The purpose of this huddle is for team members to be aware of what their colleagues are focusing on and to help one another focus on what's most important. On the next morning, each member will begin with the hit rate for the previous day, sharing how many of the three priorities were actually accomplished. "Three out of three," would be the desired response. It is important to keep the environment open, fun, and supportive so the hit rate does not become an uncomfortable part of the conversation. You will find that as people get familiar with the huddle, they will improve their ability to define their priorities and organize their day for success.

The three priorities are not the only things each team member will work on during the day. Come on, this is the real world! The three priorities are simply those tasks that will make the greatest difference and on which each person wants to focus for the day. You will want to keep the conversation moving and be sure you don't get hung up on too many details about any one person's tasks. After you have tried this for five consecutive workdays, have an evaluation huddle to discuss how well the huddles helped the team focus. Continue these huddles three to five times per week. Huddles should not be canceled just because one or two members are absent.

Sample dialogue

Sally: My three top priorities for today are to find a vendor for the new internal blog, resolve input errors we have been experiencing when taking double bookings, and I am going to work with Joe to cross-train him on the daily reports. How does that sound?

Diane: Sally, I like those and I would put the double-booking problem on the top of the list. It is driving everyone crazy.

Andrew: If selecting blog software is not your forte, why not ask IT to help with this.

Sally: Good point. I have a couple of ideas, but may ask IT to check my work and add to the list of possibilities if needed. Thanks.

Diane: OK, I'll go. Today is a day for me to get caught up on letters to consumers. I want to clear the backlog of letters and then get back to creating new templates for our agents to use when responding to consumer questions. So I have just two priorities today.

Bill: Are you going to be able to get current today? Perhaps you should do letters in the morning and templates in the afternoon so the letters don't end up taking the whole day. The agents really need better templates.

Sample questions for you to use to improve
dialogue during this huddle

- Who would like to start things off by telling everyone what three tasks they will be focusing on today?
- Does everyone agree that these are the most important tasks Sally could be doing today?
- Do you need any support or resources from the team to get these done?

- If that is not a top priority for today, when do you think it needs to be done?
- Sally, you put this on the list for a reason. Why do you believe it is important for today?
- Thanks everyone. Does anyone have any final questions or comments?
- We will let Sally consider our feedback. Who would like to go next?

The Project Momentum Huddle

Imagine your team is working on an important project. This project is not the only priority each person has to think about, but the excellent execution of this project will make a big difference to the company. Hold quick huddles to discuss the project's progress three to five times per week. Ask different team members to lead the huddle based on the project component on which you will focus. Put up a whiteboard or flip chart pad that you can huddle around to note the progress and brainstorm ideas, opportunities, and potential barriers. Leave the notes and brainstormed ideas up until items are addressed or dismissed by the team. Make these huddles active planning sessions that last five minutes or less. Stand up around the whiteboard and note assignments by name. You can also use this huddle with a project management program for larger projects. Encourage team members to meet in smaller groups and as needed to keep the project moving well.

Sample dialogue

John: The project is going well, but I am concerned about whether we will get the approval in time to order the program and get it in here for testing and training. Is there anything we can do to keep the forms moving?

Pamela: I share your concern, especially since so many people are out.

Michelle: Hey, Bob, can you help us out on this? Can you let May know that this can't sit on her desk just 'cuz she's the leader?

Bob: I'll see what I can do today and update everyone at the next huddle. What else is in our face this week?

Pamela: The specs are going fine. On track.

Alex: I should begin working on the content for the agent scripts this afternoon. I may be asking some of you to review my first draft for feedback. Expect e-mail from me in the next couple of days.

Sample questions for you to use to improve dialogue during this huddle

- Let's start off by looking at the calendar. Does anyone have any questions about the milestones coming up this week?
- Are there any tasks we can cross off?
- Are any slowdowns occurring? If so, where are they? What's causing the delays? What are your ideas for how to get things rolling again?
- What can I do to help things progress?
- What have you heard from others in the department about this project?
- Let's go over who owns the milestones for this week. Does anyone have any questions?
- Should we huddle again tomorrow?

The Celebratory Huddle

Huddles can be great vehicles for celebration and reflecting on a job well done. Grab a dozen doughnuts and call a quick huddle to share the good news of a team or company success. Acknowledge the team, with specifics, for their contributions and encourage people to share their stories. Tie the accomplishment to the company's broader goals and ask each person to talk about what helped support the success. Leaders spend much more time determining the reasons for failure than they do trying to understand why success occurs. Knowing what worked and why is equally important and useful. It is also beneficial for team members to participate in this discussion, as it will influence current projects and tasks. Celebratory huddles feel great and improve the overall energy and mood of the workplace.

Sample dialogue

Joan: Many of you have heard that we had a record sales week—$1.2 million—last week. That is amazing and especially in light of the fact that you had two people on vacation. I am most impressed that you were able to close the sales without keeping people holding on the line too long. Bringing in pizza lunches to help people take breaks and to thank them for working so hard was a nice touch too. Great job, everyone.

Tim: It sure was busy.

Joan: We never used to handle so many calls per agent. What do you think has made the difference?

Josephine: Having all the product information available online and easy to access helps speed up calls a lot. We are able to answer questions much more accurately and quickly.

Bert: I think we have better people. People who are a better fit for the role and better trained.

Michael: I don't know exactly, but it seems people have fewer questions and are more informed about the products. It seems as though they are coming to us ready to buy.

Joan: That's great and congratulations. What if we have another banner week this week? Is there anything you are going to need from me or one another?

*Sample questions for you to use to improve
dialogue during this huddle*

- What helped you and the team accomplish this success?
- How did you do it?
- Do you need any support or resources to maintain your momentum?
- What, if anything, was the largest nuisance that you had to get around?
- Thanks everyone, excellent work. Does anyone have any final questions or comments?

The Management Team Huddle

This is a great alternative to the dreaded traditional staff meeting and is ideal for a team of three to eight managers, especially for peers who rely heavily on one another. If your managers keep a traditional workweek, hold two huddles; one on Monday right after lunch and the second on Thursday morning. By the middle of Monday, most managers have an idea of what kinds of challenges and opportunities face them for the week. The Monday huddle is used to communicate and clarify each person's priorities and to get input and peer support. The Thursday huddle should be done in the morning so each member can report on what's left for the week and be able to get assistance or resources lined up to finish the week with a bang. If you wait until Friday or Thursday afternoon to hold the second huddle, your managers may not have time to help one another make anything happen before the week ends.

Sample dialogue

Jeremy: I am sure the week is already off to a brisk start. Who would like to share their top areas of focus first?

Wendy: I have been hit with several last-minute requests for employees. This week, I need to get a handle on which positions we are recruiting for now and which are most critical. I am going to be coming to you with questions about your positions and may ask for your help in determining the best place to advertise.

Garth: I think a lot of those requests came after a meeting we had discussing our third-quarter projections. They are way up and we need help to make it all happen.

Wendy: I understand, I may just need you to participate in the process a bit more if you want these positions filled right away.

Jeremy: Great, we'll be ready. Who would like to go next? Don't be shy. OK, I will go. I want to get the upgrade project detailed out and agreed to by all parties. I will be calling a work meeting with several of you for sometime tomorrow. I also need to complete my forecast for the rest of the year and cut some of the expenses to pay for the new system. I am open to any ideas, so feel free to stop by and let me know what you would do if you were in my shoes. Janice, what about you, what's on the top of your list?

Sample questions for you to use to improve dialogue during this huddle

- Who wants to go first?
- What are you most concerned about? What is keeping you up at night?
- Does anyone need quick input or ideas?
- Would it be helpful if people thought about it for the rest of the day and got back to you one-on-one? We could also do a quick end-of-day huddle if you like.
- What could we do collectively, as a management team, that would make the greatest impact this week?
- What's getting in your way?
- How do your production levels look for the week?

A Real Example

Here is an example, written in their own words, of how a hospital is using huddles (and cutting their staff meetings in half) to improve communication and focus. This excerpt comes from the *Permanente Journal*, an online newsletter.

Staff Empowerment, A Prescription For Success
by Cynthia R. Copp, MSN, APRN, CPNP;
Christine Agpaoa, CMA; Sandra Carvalho;
William F. Pfeiffer, MD

Communication

For any relationship to flourish, it must include a vital component: communication. To disseminate information to the staff, two special communication avenues were set up in our clinic: our daily "morning huddle" and our semimonthly team meetings.

The "morning huddle," as we call it, is the informal daily meeting of medical assistants, registered nurses, and nurse practitioners who are working in the clinic that day. They meet at the nurses' station from about 8:45 A.M. until about 9:00 A.M. to share any new forms, equipment, protocols, or pertinent information that may affect the workflow. Someone reads aloud the names of the physicians staffing the clinic that day, the medical assistants assigned to work for those practitioners, and the role of each registered nurse on the team. At the end of each morning huddle, a motivational quote is read to create a positive tone for the rest of the day.

Initially, when our health care team started, we found that meeting weekly was important so as to maintain our momentum and vigilance in formulating our principles. Then, as our team moved forward and much of the groundwork was completed, the members decided that such frequent meetings were no longer necessary but that having regular meetings at least twice monthly was important.

Part Three

ZOOM IN

Collimation is the property of laser light allowing it to stay as a tight, confined beam for large distances. It can be thought of as the "spread" in a beam of light (called divergence). This property of laser light makes it possible to use the laser as a level in construction or to pinpoint speeders on a highway.

—Mark Csele

Think of a flashlight. The light beam spreads out as it leaves the head of the flashlight and gets weaker as it travels. According to the inverse square law, each time the distance from the light doubles, its intensity decreases by a factor of four. Double the distance, quarter the intensity. Lasers are different. Laser light travels narrow and long. It jets out from the source as a parallel beam and spreads little. Photons that are not aligned to the axis of the laser tube bounce into the wall and do not make it into the exiting beam.

This focused beam can cut through barriers without damaging neighboring assets and hit a distant bull's-eye.

The third goal of the laser-focus model is zooming in to create a narrow space for the energy and conversation to travel. At one end of a laser cylinder, a tiny optical opening emits the energized beam. This small aperture concentrates the efforts of the laser beam and allows it to travel long and strong. What would this look like applied in an organization?

In the workplace, overwhelming tasks, ambiguity, and multi-tasking are deadly. They sap even the best and brightest employees of their energy, passion, and drive. Twenty years ago, spending the weekend getting organized, buying a new planner, and attending a time management class went a long way toward solving the prob-lem of getting more done with less time and resources. The "do more with less" paradigm is tired and no longer relevant now, and it is time to put it out to pasture. There are simply too many good choices and projects to introduce! As supermarket shelves bulge with more than a hundred types of cereal, business has become ac-customed to departmental plans with dozens of goals on which leaders can't possibly execute. Companies are taking on far too many tasks and implementing few plans well. This is a strategy for disaster, and leaders have the opportunity and responsibility to stop it. Zooming in involves breaking this destructive cycle and deliver-ing extraordinary results with fewer goals.

This part of the model is likely to provoke the greatest resis-tance. Most organizations are in denial about what they can carry out effectively and many have no idea of the riches that await those that go an inch wide and mile deep. Many leaders know that they are agreeing to too much, but feel powerless to change the "do more" company culture. And the crud rolls downhill as leaders spread the same flawed gospel within the organization. Each layer mimics the one above, creating a vast and complicated network of victim conversations that dam up progress and passion. These are the conversations that everyone knows about but few bring up at staff meetings. They are examples of business farce and absurdity. This section offers managers and leaders suggestions about how to zoom in on the best work in even the toughest environments, the most resistant conditions, and in the face of vigorous victim conversations. Laser-focused leaders go beyond the usual prioritizing to allow their teams to excel.

Most leaders struggle with how to best use their own time and that of their teams. Time is your currency; when you give a project time, you are communicating that it is valuable and worthwhile. But no one has enough time to dedicate to every worthy project, and going an inch deep and a mile wide will dilute your efforts and make success more elusive. When leaders focus like a laser beam, they create connection and alignment that is missing when they manage their days based on tasks and appointments. Laser focus will allow you to cut through the nice-to-do projects and zoom in on the few tasks that will make the greatest difference.

8

STOP MULTITASKING, START CHUNKING

Even in the face of the mounting scientific and anecdotal evidence (not to mention individual blood pressure and stress levels) that multitasking doesn't work, companies cling to it like shipwrecked survivors to flotsam. They believe that asking employees to multitask saves them money and time when chances are good that it will do neither.

—Megan Santosus, "Why More Is Less,"
CIO Magazine, September 2003

In a Nutshell

In most companies, the pace of work is hectic and spastic. Leaders juggle myriad projects and tasks at once. Multitasking, or trying to do many things at once, has become the norm. Unfortunately, multitasking is not the solution for coping with numerous priorities; instead, it wrecks focus and productivity. Studies confirm the downside of multitasking. Leaders want to do more with less, but when they multitask, they end up doing *less* with less. When attention is jolted from one thing to the next, they lose time during the interruption and take more time to get back up to speed and return to the task. If leaders are interrupted several times an hour, they end up losing a couple of hours every day.

Chunking helps leaders focus while allowing them to be responsive. Chunking means carving out segments of time that you will use to focus on one thing. You should strive to schedule and enjoy several focusing chunks per week. To enjoy the benefits of chunking, you will need to schedule time chunks in advance and exercise resolve to ensure these precious time blocks do not get consumed by interruptions or diversions.

Multitasking is thought to be a way to do more with less. Jobs are combined and workers have an increasingly broad array of tasks that need to be done in one day. Project managers juggle several projects at once. Many leaders sense there must be a better way but fail to focus on a solution because they, too, are multitasking. The trouble is, when you multitask, you cannot do more with less. You end up doing less with less.

Many researchers and experts agree that multitasking carries hidden costs. Joshua Rubinstein, David Meyer, and Jeffrey Evans, three Ph.D. researchers from the Federal Aviation Administration and the University of Michigan at Ann Arbor, studied patterns in time lost when workers switched repeatedly between two tasks of varying complexity and familiarity. In four experiments, subjects moved between tasks such as solving math problems or categorizing objects. The researchers measured the subjects' performance speeds in different scenarios. They found that for all types of tasks, subjects lost time when they had to switch from one task to another, and time costs increased with the complexity of the tasks. What this means is that when your employees are interrupted, they lose time and efficiency in two ways. First, the diversion itself takes them away from the task. Second, to get back into the task, they need to warm up their thinking and refamiliarize themselves with where they left off. In a busy work environment, chances are good that these interruptions will occur multiple times per hour and cause a significant reduction in focus and productivity.

Creativity expert and University of Chicago professor of psychology Mihaly Csikszentmihalyi warns that multitasking hinders attention and energy:

> Thus one of the fashionable concepts of high-tech companies, "multitasking," is more myth than a reality. Humans cannot really successfully multitask, but can rather move attention rapidly from one task to the other in quick succession, which only makes us feel as if we were actually doing things simultaneously. However, this strategy is not as effective as is widely believed. It takes anywhere from

fifteen minutes to an hour to get one's mind around a difficult problem, to establish the conditions to develop a worthwhile solution. If one switches too soon and too often from one task to the next, it is likely that what the mind will come up with is going to be superficial, if not trivial [2004, p. 77].

> *Key Point:* Leaders are told they need to do more with less, but when they multitask, they end up doing less with less, and thinking less. Precious time and energy are lost.

In a September 2003 *CIO Magazine* article called "Why More Is Less," Megan Santosus wrote:

> Not only does {multitasking] take a personal toll on employees, it also doesn't work. . . . Darrel Raynor, a managing director with Data Analysis & Results, has been aware of multitasking's damaging effects on productivity for a number of years. Raynor, who works with companies to create project management offices as a way of boosting IT productivity, says a database analyst asked to switch among four projects will likely be 45 percent less productive than if she's allowed to finish one before starting the next.

A loss of 45 percent productivity is significant and means that you would need roughly two analysts to accomplish what one could do if not multitasking. Most project managers (leaders are also project managers) face the challenge of managing multiple programs while trying to work in the most efficient way. Educator, scientist, and author Eli Goldratt also stressed the downside of multitasking on throughput in his bestselling book, *Critical Chain* (1997): "'Multitasking is probably the biggest killer of lead time,' I say. 'And we all suffer from it.' Call it meetings, call it emergencies, call it other jobs. The impact is the same. Lead time inflates" (p. 126).

Are there ways you can line up projects to optimize productivity and throughput? The research shows that having employees work on one project at a time is best. But is this realistic? Multitasking seems inevitable given today's hectic work pace, and perhaps this is why few leaders have been able to achieve laser focus. In *The Right Decision Every Time* (2005), business leader and MIT Sloan School Scholar Luda Kopeikina called multitasking a "Death Habit," and offered this mini-rant:

> In the current business environment, where there is more work in each job position than can be handled, we are taught to multitask. Conventional wisdom says, "Never lose a moment—if you are talking on the phone, scan your e-mails at the same time." The result is that we never have time to focus! This habit is in sharp contrast to the behavior that peak performers in sports train to achieve. Successful athletes know that when every physical and mental resource is focused, your power to perform multiplies tremendously. . . . The habit of multitasking splinters our resources and prevents us from developing and executing at peak performance levels [p. 18].

To perform at your best, you need to learn to focus your resources. The first step toward moving away from multitasking is to admit that it is not an effective way to work. In a June 2002 article in *Harvard Management Update*, Jennifer McFarland suggests leaders take multitasking off the pedestal: "You can't always avoid having to tend to half a dozen matters within a space of an hour, but if you continue to view such occasions as the managerial ideal instead of a necessary evil, you'll never make any improvements."

If multitasking wrecks focus and productivity, what is a leader to do? In some companies, leaders would be laughed out of the building if they suggested employees work on only one task at a time. Furthermore, they would not be willing to let people ignore e-mail, phone calls, meetings, and other normal business exchanges. Some calls and e-mail messages need to be addressed right away.

Key Point: Multitasking does not work and it is not an efficient way to focus or produce results. Doing one task at a time is not realistic, either.

Chunking

Multitasking wastes time, energy, and concentration, but it is a natural outcrop of today's busy work environment and broader job descriptions. You are not going to change these things overnight, but you can begin helping yourself and your employees achieve greater focus and productivity by implementing chunking. Chunking combines the benefits of focusing on one thing with the needs for workers to do various tasks during the day. In *The Effective Executive*, management expert Peter Drucker writes of the importance of dedicating large chunks of time to important tasks:

> In every executive job, a large part of the time must therefore be wasted on things which, though they apparently have to be done, contribute nothing or little. Yet most of the tasks of the executive require, for minimum effectiveness, a fairly large quantum of time. To spend in one stretch less than this minimum is sheer waste. One accomplishes nothing and has to begin all over again. . . . To be effective, every knowledge worker, and especially every executive, therefore needs to be able to dispose of time in fairly large chunks. To have dribs and drabs of time at his disposal will not be sufficient even if the total is an impressive number of hours [2002, p. 29].

Chunking means carving out segments of time that you will use to focus on one thing. Turn off your cell phone, set your office phone to take messages, and shut down e-mail. Let your team members and colleagues know you need to focus. For that precious period of time, you want to direct all your energies and thoughts to one task, plan, or project. Chunks of time vary in length. Ideally, you will want to set aside a full day, half day, or a block of one or two hours. Longer chunks are better. In a week's time, you should try to focus for one half-day chunk, three two-hour chunks, and several one-hour chunks.

Do you find it difficult to disconnect for two or four hours? Imagine you are in a meeting. You can't answer e-mail messages or phone calls (or you shouldn't). Talk to your staff and make sure they know when you have set aside chunks. Encourage them to do the same and help them rearrange their day to enable chunking. Make chunking a regular practice and you will find that people get used to it and learn when to engage one another and when to allow them to focus. It's a beautiful thing!

> *Key Point:* Chunking allows leaders to focus, get more accomplished, and be responsive to people and information.

Chunking is not a system. You do not need to attend a class to begin using chunking to focus. You just need to set time aside to focus and eliminate distractions. The most important skill needed to use chunking is resolve. You will need to resist the temptation to allow chunks of time to dissipate when daily office brush fires beckon. You might even need to change your location or context to escape interruptions. You might need to talk to your employees, peers, and manager about how you intend to use chunking and ask for their support. Do whatever it takes. Your work is too important to let it fall victim to multitasking.

> *Key Point:* Chunking requires resolve, but the benefits are worth the effort.

For most leaders, the day is so busy that it can become a blur. They rush from one thing to the next and endure several interruptions along the way. Technology has made it possible for leaders to be interrupted in more ways and places. Few experience peace and focus. Chunking is a practice that will allow you to focus on what's important while meeting the demands of today's caffeinated work climate.

In the Real World

Give chunking a try! Here are several suggestions for how to use chunking to increase focus, a sample schedule, and a workplace fable about multitasking.

Ways to Chunk. At first, you might be hesitant to tell team members or peers to leave you alone between 2 and 4 P.M. There are ways you can begin to use chunking that will prevent you from coming across as cold or uncaring. Try these techniques:

- Talk to your team and peers about the downside of multitasking and let them know you want to give chunking a try. Share this chapter and encourage them to join you.

- Help those around you know when you do not want to be disturbed. Publish your schedule and include focus chunks.

- Use a friendly sign to indicate you need to focus. If you work in an office, put a discreet sign on your door. Close the door when chunking. If you work in a cubicle or open space, post a sign that asks coworkers and visitors not to disturb you. Some people who work in cubicles string a sign across the opening of their space to let people know they are chunking. Others have used a conservative curtain on an expandable rod to close off distractions.

- Don't chunk halfway by leaving your e-mail active and phones on. E-mail notifications can be very distracting. It might be tough to do this, but give it a try and you will find that shutting down your e-mail program for two hours is liberating.

- Start with modest one- or two-hour chunks and work your way toward using chunks of four, six, or eight hours.

- Block chunks of time on your calendar. It is too easy for a leader's schedule to get filled with multiple meetings. Mark out your chunks as though they were important meetings that you cannot and do not want to miss. They are!

- Help your team members focus by assigning tasks and projects with chunking in mind. Do not expect that people will jump from one task to the next throughout the day. Don't assign a new task if you know someone is concentrating on finishing important work. Time the work and manage it so it flows more effectively. Manage your commitments to your peers and managers to ensure that you do not get in the way of your employees' focus and productivity.

Sample Schedule Using Chunking. Chunking works best when you schedule blocks of time in advance. Even though your schedule might change, it is better to schedule twenty chunking hours and achieve ten hours than to struggle to take a few hours to focus after your schedule has filled up. It is also helpful to create some regularity with your schedule when possible. This helps people learn when you are available and when you wish to be left undisturbed. Here is a sample chunking schedule:

Day	*Morning*	*Morning*	*Afternoon*	*Afternoon*
Monday	8:00–10:00		1:00–2:00	
Tuesday	8:00–9:00		1:00–2:00	2:00–4:00
Wednesday	8:00–9:00		1:00–2:00	
Thursday	8:00–9:00		1:00–2:00	
Friday	8:00–9:00		1:00–2:00	2:00–4:00

This schedule includes fifteen hours of chunking. Some of those time slots will not work out, but imagine what you could accomplish if you were able to focus for even eight of these hours. Friday afternoons are great times to use chunking to focus. There are fewer scheduled meetings and it feels great to end the week on a high!

Coyote Tries Multitasking

Here is an amusing but helpful blog post in the form of a fable from *The Coyote Within*, by Adrian Savage (2005):

> One day, Coyote was having a drink after work with his friend, Fox. He was extremely tired. Work seemed to be getting harder and harder. However much he did, there always seemed to be just as much waiting for him to do.

"Sometimes I wish I could split myself in two," he said to Fox. "If there were two of me, I'd get everything done easily."

"Why not?" said Fox. "Ever heard of multitasking?"

Coyote hadn't. Fox found it hard to explain, but he did his best.

"It's like splitting yourself in two," he said. "Instead of concentrating yourself on one task, while all those other ones keep yelling for attention, you do several at once. You spread yourself a little thinner over more activities."

Coyote liked the sound of that. He's a lazy fellow, always looking for ways to save effort. Of course, Fox knew about Coyote's powers. He thought he'd have some fun at Coyote's expense.

Next day, there were two Coyotes, each one at a different meeting. Two to handle calls and emails. One to talk to customers while the other got on with administrative tasks.

"Wow," Coyote thought. "Why didn't I do this before?" By the end of the day, he'd done all his work and even got a start on the next day's quota.

Of course, there was still only one real Coyote. The two he'd split himself into couldn't make more Coyote, so each was a little thinner and less solid than the real thing. To make them, he'd had to share out his true substance.

All went well for while, until the work facing the two Coyotes built up again. The boss had noticed how much work Coyote was able to handle, so he added more.

"Oh dear," thought Coyote. "I'm back where I began. There's only one thing to do."

Now there were four Coyotes, all working hard. The boss was delighted at the increase in productivity, so he let a couple of Raccoons go and gave their work to Coyote as well.

Poor Coyote. At the end of each day, all four versions of him were exhausted. He would try to bring them back together, but he was feeling so fragmented it wasn't always possible. One or two parts of him would just wander off, leaving him feeling odd and incomplete.

Eventually, there were eight Coyotes and he didn't even try to pull them back together at the end of each day. Each one tried to live independently. The real Coyote was almost lost.

After a few months, one of the Coyotes was outside the boss's office and overheard a conversation the boss was having with the Big Chief.

"Coyote's only a shadow of his former self," the boss said. "Sure, he seems to be everywhere at once, but his work quality is poor. I don't think he's putting enough of himself into what he does. I'm probably going to let him go."

Coyote was mad. How dare his boss suggest he wasn't what he used to be, after all the extra work he'd taken on.

As he walked back to his office, Coyote—or that part of him—glanced in a mirror on the wall of the corridor. He stopped in horror. Coyote was reflected in the mirror, of course, but it wasn't the Coyote he expected. This was a pale, indistinct version. Heavens! If you looked hard, you could see right through him. He'd spread himself so thinly there was almost nothing there.

In desperation, he went to see his doctor, Owl.

"Hooo dear," Owl said. "You've been very foolish as usual, Coyote. What made you believe you could split yourself into all these parts and not have to make each one thinner and weaker?"

Coyote—or part of him, he could no longer quite recall—felt ashamed. He promised Owl he wouldn't be so stupid again and set off to collect all his parts together.

It took him quite a while. Most of them were so frail after rushing about on his behalf, they were hardly visible any more. And the work they'd been doing was as thin and weak as they were. Coyote knew he'd be blamed for that, but he guessed he deserved it.

He never tried multitasking again, whatever the pressures. He was too afraid he'd be unable to put himself back together.

9

DO ONE GREAT THING

I've learned that you can't have everything and do everything at the same time.

—Oprah Winfrey

In a Nutshell

Many leaders are dissatisfied with their results. They work hard and want to have impact, but time slips away too fast for them to stay on track. They agree to do too much and then are unable to execute well. To improve focus, leaders must change how they define what's relevant and say no much more often. You and your team can only do so many tasks well. To determine how much you should do, take a look at the quality of the work, implementation, and follow-up. It is better to do a few things well than many things poorly.

Strive to complete at least one great thing each day. Great things are the tasks you finish and the actions you take that, relative to all the things you could be doing, will make the most significant difference. Great things facilitate and enable forward progress. Imagine the impact if you and all your peer leaders did one great thing each day!

◆ ◆ ◆

Laura is a smart and motivated vice president for a growing medium-sized company. She maintains a detailed to-do list and works full tilt from the moment she gets to the office until the moment she leaves. She brings some work home, too. From meetings to planning to phone calls and e-mail to creative work, her day slips away. Her whole department works at the speed of light. But Laura lacks focus and she often leaves the office feeling as though she has not accomplished much of anything. What a tragedy! Laura is a talented and engaged leader. Any company would be lucky to have her on their leadership team. And yet she is killing herself every day and not making enough difference to the business. Her brave efforts have left Laura and her team heading for burnout.

Laura is not alone. Many hardworking leaders are frustrated and dissatisfied with their results. Many create this problem for themselves by saying yes to too many things. Way too many things. Yeses that fill their days and their team's days. Days filled to the point that many great tasks get shortchanged or pushed aside. The trouble with *yes* is that it is often applied to the wrong questions.

"Yes, we can do that."

"Yes, I will attend the meeting."

"Yes, I have a few minutes."

"Yes, that would be nice."

"Yes, we have the budget."

Questions that can be answered in these terms become the relevancy barometer for tasks that could fill a hundred to-do lists. Think about that. How many items on your to-do list are there because you can do them and they are good things to do? Talented leaders *can* do many things. This does not mean that they should. In fact, senior managers should value leadership resources and take care not to squander them on marginal work.

And the yeses roll downhill, filling up to-do lists throughout the organization until even the part-time interns can't get all their work done. When leaders agree to a project or task, they often commit their team's time and energy. Many employees do not feel comfortable managing up to ask questions about why the tasks keep coming. On way to help pare down your team's list is to ask your employees their thoughts on what they do that does not make sense or support the most important goals.

The problem of too many yeses goes beyond each leader. The overactive *yes* is an organization-wide issue, and some organizational cultures are worse than others. If someone calls a meeting that everyone knows is a waste of time, what happens? Does anyone say anything? If you attend a staff meeting that lacks relevance and impact, does anyone suggest changing or abandoning the meeting? In many organizations, it is normal to attend ineffective meetings and spend time on marginally worthwhile tasks. This is crazy, and if you want to improve focus and results, you will want to get tougher about how you spend your days. Don't endure another crummy meeting or spend another minute chasing down unimportant information! There are many more good things to do than you can complete.

> *Key Point:* Focus suffers when leaders don't say no to good but nonessential tasks.

Leaders should change how they define what's relevant and say no much more often. "Can we do that?" will lead to too many yeses. These questions will better support focus and results:

- Relative to all the things I could be doing, is this something that will have the greatest impact on the most important goals?
- Will this task improve results or effectiveness beyond what we are doing today?
- Will anyone notice if this doesn't get done?
- If I ran into a contingency today and could only do two other tasks, what would I do? Would this task still seem important?

When you change how you view relevance, you can quickly see which tasks are of marginal value. Many more things will not be relevant and should fail to make it onto the to-do list. Every day, well-meaning leaders overbook their schedules and destroy their chances for focus and optimal results. Define success as using your time in ways that add the greatest value and impact.

> *Key Point:* Task relevancy changes when you redefine success and determine what's most important.

How many tasks can you and your team do well? How many more could they do if you cut a bit of time and attention from each task? Are you serving the organization when you blaze through thirty tasks when you only have time to do eight tasks well? Of course not. Many of the best performers take on too many tasks. If you want to focus like a laser beam you will need to make the tough decision to zoom in on fewer tasks instead of zooming through more of them.

How do you know whether your team is blazing through versus focusing on important tasks? How do you assess their capacity to do great work? These are important questions because you need to know when to say yes and when to say no. Here are several indicators you can use to judge whether you or your team are taking on too many tasks:

- Are you able to create and update a plan that will support excellent results?
- Have you been able to take the time to involve the right people?
- Are you communicating appropriate updates and seeking feedback on how implementation is going?
- Have you been able to give each task the generative thinking it needs and deserves—the amount of creativity it actually warrants?
- Are you satisfied with the level of analysis you and your team are doing?

- How well are previously implemented projects being monitored and maintained?

- Are you able to spend enough time coaching and mentoring your staff?

These questions may seem like a setup; most leaders are so busy that their schedule dictates their actions. Even so, if you are not able to answer yes to these questions, it is an indication that you may be doing too many things—and doing too few of them well. Regardless of your corporate culture, doing many things pretty well will not benefit the company as much as doing a few tasks very well. This does not mean that projects should be worked on until paralysis by analysis sets in. Don't confuse this advice with a suggestion that your organization should do less or slow down.

> *Key Point:* It is better to do five things well than ten things poorly. Determine your capacity and your team's by looking at the quality and maintenance of your work.

To-do lists are part of the problem. The process of emptying your head and keeping a running list of tasks, small or large, feels satisfying. A long list means you probably aren't forgetting anything. If you can make a long list of things to do, why wouldn't you? Keeping a legal pad or PDA full of uncompleted tasks does not help you focus. Your mind will see all the tasks that need to be done and go about trying to satisfy too many needs. You don't want to be like Laura and leave at the end of a long day feeling like you did not get anything important done. Do you need a to-do list to tell you what's most important? You shouldn't need to be reminded of the ways in which you can make the greatest difference. These core tasks are likely emblazoned on your mind.

If you do use a to-do list, make it small and short. List the goals that you need to support and the precious few tasks that will best support them. At the top of this short list, write the one great thing that you want to get done today. Strive to get at least one great thing done each day. If you can do more than one, that's great, but start with doing just one. What's a great thing? Think about your role and the goals of your function and the company. What's the one thing you could do today that would best facilitate and enable the forward movement of work? What's the one barrier you could obliterate that would get things moving again? What's the one conversation you could stimulate that would leave your team energized and ready to attack a tough problem? What could you do that would help the company make better decisions about whether to approve a new system or process? What could you do that would clarify expectations, goals, or current performance? Great things will often address one of these areas. If you do at least one great thing per day, you will wind up each day feeling satisfied. Once you get to the point of doing one great thing each day, try doing one great thing each morning and each afternoon. If all leaders did two great things every day, their collective contribution to the company would be massive and transformative.

> *Key Point:* Laser-focused leaders probably don't need a to-do list. Commit to doing one great thing each day.

Some readers might think that this chapter advocates setting lower standards and lowering expectations, but the aim is quite the reverse. It is important to do more than your competition and create a fast-paced and results-oriented work environment. Your standards for quality of execution should go higher and you should raise your standards on how you and your team spend your time. This is not an easy challenge. In today's crazy work environments, focus is elusive. Days are overfilled with tasks of varying degrees of importance and impact. Laser-focused leaders know that the frenetic pace is the new normal, so they make certain that they do one or two great things each day, and they get comfortable with saying no.

In the Real World

Culling a long to-do list is not easy. Focusing like a laser beam requires discipline, toughness, and a stricter definition of relevance.

Here are several ideas that can help you spend more time doing great things.

Seven Times to Say No

Leaders need to say no to wrong things and even to many good things. Here are seven common opportunities to improve focus by saying no. When you first start saying no, expect a puzzled reaction. But stick with it; once people see how well you can focus, they will understand and may even follow suit. (Wouldn't that be nice!)

• *When you don't think you should attend a meeting:* Talk to the meeting leader and make it clear that your first priority right now is [whatever it happens to be]. Reinforce that you would be happy to be on call for any issues that come up and that need your input.

• *When meetings are not effective:* Be honest and resolve to not sit through another bad meeting. Share your observations with the group. Acknowledge that everyone is busy and you are concerned that this meeting is not a good use of time. Request that the meeting agenda be changed, the frequency reduced, or the meetings be canceled altogether. Organizations have many ways to keep people in the loop. If your manager is the meeting leader, have a private conversation before the meeting. Chances are your manager is feeling the same way as you.

• *Someone is proposing new tasks or projects that you don't think deserve the resources required:* Ask the individual or team considering this work whether this task, relative to everything else going, will make a big difference to the company's goals. If they say the task should be top priority, ask what project should be taken off the priority list.

• *Your manager wants everyone to do new detailed weekly reports and you think this is a waste of time:* Ask your manager what unfilled need the report will serve. Make it clear that you are concerned about spending the time to document detailed activities instead of doing them, and ask if there are other ways that you could meet the need. Often you will be able to get your manager to compromise a bit.

- *You have been asked to check out an idea from a recent trade magazine article:* Let the person know that, while it sounds interesting, you do not want to get sidetracked or distracted from your focus this week. Offer to ask an intern to do some research when there's time, but make no commitments as to when this will be. Often, the requestor will just drop the idea.

- *You have been asked to do something and you don't feel you are the right person for the task:* Poor role clarity, delegation, and empowerment can wreck focus. Talk to the person about why you do not think that you or your team members are appropriate for this task.

- *You have been asked to multitask during a time that you need to focus:* Focus time is precious time! While emergencies may occur, protect your time from everyday interruptions by nicely asking people to chat later and letting people know when you will be available.

But beware of these wimpy ways to say no. Avoid them all, as they will make you seem weak and unsure of yourself.

- "I am not taking on new responsibilities." This is weak because you *would* add a high-priority task to your list. Don't say this when what you really mean is that *this task* is not important.

- "I don't have room in my calendar." This is weak because it speaks more to your inability to manage your calendar than the task. If the task were important, you would make room in your calendar.

- "I cannot do this now, but I can do it later." This might be weak if it is just an excuse to avoid a confrontation about the task. If the task is not a good use of time, don't offer to do it later. If the task is a good use of your time, then go ahead—but be clear about when you can complete it.

The Three Rights Filter

Here is a tool you can use to evaluate whether a task should go on your short and focused to-do list. It is called the Three Rights Filter, which stands for right task, right time, right place.

Filter #1—Right Task—asks whether this is the right work. Should we be spending our time on this? Many tasks should not make it through this filter. Does it make it through?

If yes, go to Filter #2—Right Time, which asks if this is the right time to be doing this. Does this go above other priorities? Many tasks should not make it through this filter. Does it make it through?

If yes, go to Filter #3—Right Place, which asks who should be doing this. Most tasks should not end up on *your* list.

After you apply this filter, you do one of four things with each task:

- Get rid of it: The task did not make it through the first filter, and no one should do it.
- Do it: This task goes on your list.
- Delegate or assign it: The task should be done by someone else.
- Modify it: The scope, size, or timing of the task needs changes. Then the task goes onto the proper list, which may or may not be yours.

Distinguishing Good Things and Great Things

Here is a blog post from Management Craft that offers specific thoughts on the type of leadership tasks that might make it on the good to-do list (but really shouldn't be done) and great to-do lists (the ones that need action).

Managing Outside the Box
By Lisa Haneberg

There's a powerful pull, like a gravitational pull, that keeps many managers from making a difference. It's the management box.

Here's what's inside the box:

- Meetings
- Administrivia
- To-do lists and piles

- Routine tasks
- Handling daily brushfires
- Taking care of people's problems
- Monitoring performance

These things in the box can fill our days, but we can't let them. This is not why we became managers and it is not what our companies most need from us.

Outside the box:

- Breakthroughs in alignment
- Dialogue that enlivens the workplace
- Seizing opportunity
- Collaboration that improves the business
- Barrier obliteration

It may seem hard to step outside the box because bosses and employees reinforce in-box management. That's ironic, because they seek the results and feeling of out-of-box management. They just don't know, and this creates a vicious circle of reinforcement of the wrong things.

How to step outside the box:

Step outside the box one foot at a time. Align the workplace, change what you do daily, and improve dialogue. Say no to sucky meetings. *Say no to sucky meetings*. **Say no to sucky meetings**. Until you do, the pull of the box will be tough to overcome.

Are you a senior leader? Talk to your management team today, in the next hour. Tell them about the box and give them your blessing to step outside. Better yet, realign your expectations such that you do not reinforce in-box management.

Not sure how to begin? Print out this post, take it to your OD department and ask them to help drive the migration. If they do not know what to do, get a new OD department, this is basic stuff.

Yeah, let's not make this complicated, this is simple. The pull is strong but as soon as you get away from the force, managing outside the box is very simple.

10

LET GO

It is not necessary to change. Survival is not mandatory.
—W. Edwards Deming

Faced with the choice between changing one's mind and proving that there is no need to do so, almost everyone gets busy on the proof.
—John Kenneth Galbraith

In a Nutshell

Companies and individuals must evaluate whether strategies, goals, projects, and tasks remain relevant. Remember, relevance is based on your definition of success. When you change, or your company does, goals and projects that were once relevant may no longer serve success. Laser focus can only be achieved if you stop doing some things. Many people hold on to goals too long. Goals change. Preferences change. Passions and interests change. Hanging on to obsolete goals saps energy and focus.

Neither companies nor individuals should waste time and energy focusing on the wrong things. It is critical to change or discontinue projects that no longer make sense or are not working. The time and resources used to support or maintain obsolete plans, goals, and projects can and should be put to better use. Leaders can improve their focus and results by periodically realigning goals, projects, and processes.

◆ ◆ ◆

On the cover of the Campbell's Soup Company's 2001 annual report was a simple Andy Warhol rendition of the red-and-white can and the words, "It is not enough to be a legend." Americans' preferences for soups change every year and the company's leaders know they must respond to ensure the continued and long-term success of the brand that many generations grew up with.

Being a legend and relevant is not easy. Over the years, the company has shifted its focus away from declining selections and over to new products. Consumers want a more portable soup, so Campbell's now offers a microwaveable line of products. More Americans value organic ingredients, and the company has responded with organic broth selections. It now sells premium refrigerated soups to meet the growing interest in gourmet foods. As tastes change, the company's products must shift. When the low-carb diet craze hit, Campbell's introduced a line of soups called Carb Request. That line has since been discontinued, mirroring America's waning interest in strict low-carbohydrate eating. The company also discontinued its Campbell's Classics line to give more shelf space to the brands and flavors that consumers preferred.

Shelf space is like real estate, and the quantity and selection of products is in a constant state of flux. Preferences differ by region, too. Pepper Pot soup is popular along the East Coast; Asian-inspired soups are sought in the West. Packaging is also important. Campbell's has moved away from packaging products in glass containers because consumers want a lighter and safer container. Aseptic containers are increasingly popular. To remain successful, Campbell's Soup, like all businesses, needs to let go of some products to make way for innovations and focus on what consumers want to buy.

Every company must evaluate its products and let go of them when they no longer serve the organization. In the summer of 2005, Apple discontinued its popular iPod Mini line of music players and replaced them with a new smaller and more powerful souped-up product called iPod Nano. Even though sales of the iPod Mini were brisk, Apple felt it appropriate to let go of the product to enable focus on its remaining three models of music and video players, the iPod, iPod Shuffle, and the new iPod Nano. Around the same time, Apple also let go of a special U2 version of the iPod.

In October 2005, Delta Air Lines announced that it would end its discount carrier, Song. Song Airlines had been created by Delta in 2002 to compete against low-cost carriers such as Southwest and JetBlue. With capital-intensive operations like airlines, making decisions to add or subtract service takes significant consideration and consumes many resources. Delta decided the company was better off refocusing its efforts. "As Delta continues its transformation to become a more customer-focused airline, we are incorporating the best of Song into the best of Delta," Gerald Grinstein, Delta's chief executive officer, said in a statement posted on the Delta Web site.

These are the stories you read about in business magazines, but they are the tip of the iceberg of what organizations should question. The same scenario needs to occur within the organization. Do projects, processes, or tasks no longer serve the goals of the company? Have goals become obsolete? Do you still parade the same mission and vision statements every planning cycle when people know that these words don't describe what's important to the company? When you fail to acknowledge and let go of obsolete goals and projects, they muck up everyone's ability to think clearly and execute well.

> *Key Point:* Projects, products, processes, and tasks need to be questioned and discontinued when they do not support focus and results.

Your individual goals change, too. Do you know how to recognize when your heart and mind has shifted away from the goals you set out to achieve? Many people hold on to goals too long. You cannot be successful or focused if you measure accomplishments against an outdated set of goals or expectations. It is important to recognize that aspirations you had in the past may not matter much to you today. For example, many leaders find that as they mature, participating in exciting projects becomes more important than getting promotions. Others will begin their career aiming to lead a large organization but then shift to wanting to start their own small company. The work that interests you might change as well. Some leaders seek management roles only to discover that research and development is more interesting. Some avoid management but then find it extremely satisfying once they experience its intrinsic rewards. Maybe you believe you want to get an advanced degree but find that your heart just is not into making the necessary commitment.

> *Key Point:* Goals change. Hanging on to obsolete goals saps energy and focus. It is critical to change or discontinue projects that no longer make sense or are not working.

Why are leaders reluctant to cut loose from an outdated project or goal? Time, energy, and resources have been spent, and it is tough to let that go or to admit the effort has been wasted. Perhaps the project is not a complete waste of resources, but is no longer a top priority. Maybe the project was once very important and people would feel unsettled giving it up. Expert executive coach Marshall Goldsmith echoed the struggle some leaders experience in an online article called "Let it Go" (2005): "While our personal commitment usually leads to more success, it can make it extremely hard for us to change. The more committed we are to a strategy, the harder it is for us to realize it is the wrong strategy."

Here's the thing. Most companies do not have the luxury of investing in marginal projects. If a project is not central to meeting the company's goals or is no longer a top priority, you need to question whether it should be continued at all.

All goals and projects, even those that you do not actively work on, take up energy and focus. They are in the back of your mind and occupy a stack on your desk. These goals attend meetings with you even if they are never brought up in conversation. Obsolete goals and projects nag at leaders like overdue bills. The same holds true for personal goals. You think about them now and then and lament that you are not making the progress you had hoped. Instead of worrying about getting back to that goal, perhaps it is time to determine if it is still important. Once you make the decision to let go, a burden is lifted and you can use the energy to focus on what really matters now.

> *Key Point:* The time and resources used to support or maintain obsolete plans, goals, and projects can and should be put to better use.

Leaders can improve their focus and results by periodically realigning goals, projects, and processes. You want your actions to support and be consistent with what's most important today and for the future. Evaluating the relevancy of your goals and projects will help you uncover opportunities to reduce stress and waste. It is stressful when you know that you are not paying attention to a goal that you once held dear. It might be difficult to acknowledge that the goal is no longer relevant or helpful, but doing so is necessary. You can free up mental and physical energy by taking stock of your goals and letting go where appropriate.

Within the organization, it is critical to review and let go of obsolete goals and projects. You should evaluate the relevancy of the work at least quarterly and when business conditions change. When you let go of a project, goal, or process, you may feel a collective sigh of relief from your team. Your team wants to know that the work they are doing matters and ties to the goals of the company. When employees sense that their efforts are being wasted, it causes frustration and lowers motivation and morale. Leaders who regularly realign their team's work improve focus, results, and satisfaction.

> *Key Point:* You should realign goals and actions periodically.

What if you cannot change a goal that no longer inspires enthusiasm? People sometimes fall in and out of love with ideas, objectives, and projects many times. Does this make these goals obsolete? It is important to distinguish between goals that you should let go and those you need to reenergize. To do this in the workplace, realign to the overall goals of your company. For personal goals, you need to reevaluate the future you want to create for yourself and your family. If the goal remains important, then you need to reenergize its support and alignment.

Austrian neurologist and psychiatrist Viktor Frankl wrote about his experiences as a concentration camp inmate in *Man's Search for Meaning*. Part of his struggle was to constantly redefine his response to the conditions given his inability to change them. He wrote, "When we are no longer able to change a situation, we are challenged to change ourselves" (1997 [1946], p. 135). Most leaders will not have to deal with situations as difficult as Frankl's, but their focus will benefit from similar thinking. Sometimes you need to let go of your current assumptions and opinions about a goal or project so you can get aligned and focus appropriately.

> *Key Point:* When you can't change the circumstances, change the way you see and act on them.

Letting go frees up your mind and energy. It is easier to focus like a laser beam when you zoom in only on those things that are most important for success.

In the Real World

In what ways should you let go? Here is a story, a few suggestions and a fascinating and inspirational blog post about letting go.

A True Story

Forty-five middle managers convened for a day of management training. They worked for an admired advertising and marketing firm. Their workplace was fast-paced and creative. Competition in their market segment was fierce. They needed to be better and faster than the other players. As a result, alignment to goals was critical.

One of their problems was lack of clarity about what was most important. The CEO was a charismatic communicator who addressed the management team in various ways including regular roundtable meetings, via e-mail, by weekly video, and at team meetings. The problem was that he communicated so many messages over time that it was unclear which were still relevant. One participant offered the following written comment in a pretraining survey: "What happened to the emphasis on the five priorities for 2005? We have a tendency to focus on the 'flavor of the month' and shoot at scattered targets rather than staying the course." And during the training, several middle managers brought up the same point, saying they were unsure whether the priorities had changed. They did not know which priorities they should apply today. These managers needed help determining where to let go and where to focus.

As a leader, you expect people to hear what you communicate and manage their piece of the business in alignment with this. As your messages change, circle back to previous messages and clarify which priorities remain pertinent to today's goals.

Knowing When to Let Go

Here is a chart that offers questions you can use to determine when it is time to let go of a goal, project, process, or task.

Focus applied to. . . .	Questions
Personal Goals	In what work are you most interested? List all the goals you have set for yourself. How many of these goals are you really committed to accomplishing? Why are these goals on the list and which of them are you most passionate about? If you observed your actions, what would you think are your priorities? How have your goals and priorities changed in the last year?

Organization Goals	Are the vision and mission still relevant and useful in enabling focus and alignment? What goals have you communicated to employees? Are these goals still relevant? How have the needs and opportunities of the business changed? How should this be reflected in the goals that you say are top priority? Which goals would best serve the organization? Do you have the capacity to focus like a laser beam on all your goals? If not, which goals can you set aside?
Organization Projects	List all the projects on which people are working. Do all these projects support your most important priorities? Are there any projects that were once important but seem less important now? If you had to cut half the projects, which would you eliminate? Do you have the capacity to execute well on all these projects? If not, where do you either need more resources or fewer projects? Is there a project that many people doubt is worth the effort?
Organization Processes	Given your most important priorities, which work processes most and least support the organization's success? Why? What frustrates people on a regular basis? Where are operations least efficient and focused? In what ways have the processes become bottlenecks?
Work Tasks	Take a look at what's on the department's collective to-do list. Which tasks do not directly support the highest priorities? Are there tasks that don't seem to be missed when skipped (like a staff meeting, or running a report, for example)? If the team could only do half the tasks assigned, which would you eliminate?

Focus Schmocus

A blog post from Crossroads Dispatches, by Evelyn Rodriguez

Day 6. "One of the greatest gifts is to recognize when you're in the wrong place, or doing the wrong things, then find the courage to stop whatever that is and make a change without guilt or regret" (Adrian Savage's *The Coyote Within*, "Quitting Time").

- Sometimes people say they want X. Or X is supposed to be what they want because their parents want it, their spouse, all of their culture says X is a good goal. And maybe for a while X really is their goal. But people change, priorities change.

- And now they put much of their energy in Y. In fact, Y actually becomes the new goal—but they haven't admitted to themselves and others that they've lost interest in X.

- So if you ask them they are total *failures* at accomplishing X. They obviously aren't focused enough.

- But they don't notice the singular focus they do have is on Y. They have focus. But it's on Y, not X. They are accomplishing and getting somewhere with Y.

- Perhaps in your book, you can have people note where they really are applying their energy, time, resources, effort, concern. Maybe they aren't as scattered as they believe. . . .

If you must muster the will to whip a dead horse to focus and execute, maybe that's your cue, maybe it's quitting time. I find it hard to believe people aren't applying themselves in any endeavor whatsoever (if so, they are probably suffering from depression; even the "dark night of the soul" is definitely not passive). It just may not be what you last said or last promised. Look closely, even at unpaid work and tasks if there is energy and execution there. . . .

I'm reminded of a lesson from my old philosophy professor. He used to say that the person is a crossroads. They are where the vertical line of spirituality crosses the horizontal line of practicality (apologies for my atrocious paraphrase).

I'm fully aware that I have come across as a flake, a bailer a million times. I should have seen clearly where my shifting passions were heading, but I didn't. Or that these weren't even new shifts but the primordial ground of all my passions all along.

My teacher told me that after about a year and a half of intense interest in psychology as a major in college, all of a sudden that interest fell by the wayside. Not a calculated decision as much as it was simply over. Done, clean, complete. A step perhaps. But also history. It was such a relief to hear that from someone I wholly respect as I'm discarding ideas, interests, and things faster than a snake sheds skins.

Yet in the last few years, I've never stood up a friend that I'd made a commitment to meet. I say no if I mean no and I say no a lot. Anthony de Mello was asked if he wanted to go to a movie by a friend. Thanks, but no, he answered. His friend pressed him. De Mello simply wanted to spend time by himself. And his friend was outraged because it didn't seem like a good enough reason to thwart his offer. For many people, it's easier to say maybe, or let's play it by ear than to be totally straightforward. Being straight can get you into hot water and it's easier to skirt that by anticipating what you think the other person wants to hear. That's what the escape-a-date cell phone feature is all about. Flaky—heck, that's full-fledged people-pleasing that's ultimately worse than a flat out no, I'd rather clip my toenails—or, there's clearly no match here, so why waste a lovely evening politely pretending there will ever be a second date. Try it, you might find it liberating.

11

CONCLUSION

The show begins and you feel a rush of sensuous stimulation. Swashes of vivid color dance and fly at all corners of your eyes. The lights play hide-and-seek to reveal intriguing scenes and painted people. The music is full and intricate and pushes out any unrelated thoughts you might have had. Five, ten, maybe twenty performers are each doing their own thing flawlessly and simultaneously. It's chaotic but perfectly choreographed. The air buzzes and hums, and you can feel and smell the passion. You feel the chills of excitement. Looking around, you can see that others are amazed too. Your visual field is so stimulated you cry.

Each Cirque du Soleil show offers a unique example of laser focus. The entire experience is supercharged; on stage, backstage, and in the jazzed inner souls of those sitting in the audience. Fun, intrigue, and whimsy are duplicated hundreds of times each show. For the performers, though, this is also deadly serious work. Implementation must be and is flawless. The environment is personal and everyone feels part of the show. As the audience responds, the performers respond. When the performers respond, the audience responds. The synergistic give-and-take makes this everyone's show. The verbal and nonverbal dialogue is tuned to tell the stories of this fantasy world in a way that feels real. Many distinct voices come together to create a single impression. All aspects of the show zoom in on just a few key themes and messages, with no wasted effort, no waste of space, time, or emotion. Everything fits and serves the overall vision. Cirque du Soleil focuses like a laser beam.

How does your work environment feel? Are people super-charged and engaged in their work? Do you have stimulating and relevant conversations every day? How choosy are you about how you and your team spend their time? The ten suggestions offered in this book will help you improve focus and results. Did the chapters seem like odd pairings? What does focus have to do with laughter, breathing exercises, huddles, and chunking? Conventional leadership books and training don't mention these things. Consider this description of laser focus:

- Performing work in ways that lead to high-velocity success, satisfaction, and efficiency.
- Connecting today's reality and tomorrow's goal with the straightest, most direct line of effort and resources.
- Smoothly hitting the bull's eye, and only the bull's eye.
- Jazz, peace, tango, carol, applause.

A good laugh, deep breath, or electric conversation has the power to transform work and thrust it forward. Laser focus is a way of leading, not an organizational quick fix. You can gradually improve on each of the ten areas to enjoy big benefits.

Throughout the book, the word *relevance* appears many times. Relevance is related to how you define success. An important fundamental of laser focus is learning how to define what's relevant in a way that helps you make choices that best serve your goals. The concept of relevance can change how you view your job. Explore these questions: Why does your role exist? Why are you here? As illustrated throughout the book, these questions have both low-threshold answers and high-threshold answers.

Low:

- I am here to run this department.
- My role exists to manage projects.
- I am here to manage my team and track work progress.

- My role exists to support company goals.

High:

- I am here to make a positive contribution to the business that would not occur without me. I must make a difference every day.

- My role exists to link strategy and implementation so my department optimally supports the success of the company.

- I am here to improve the effectiveness of the team and of the department's processes. Each day, week, month, and year, the capacity of the people and processes should grow.

- My role exists to see that the company's resources—people, capital, systems, processes—are not wasted on lower-yield activities. As a leader, I need to help the organization focus.

Do you see how adopting the high-threshold answers would lead to different views of what's relevant? Define success in a way that zooms in on what's most important. As you discuss options at meetings and make daily decisions, ask yourself whether they are relevant. Encourage an open conversation about where the threshold for relevancy should be placed in your organization.

Relevancy is like laser collimation; it provides direction and precision. Remember how this exploration of focus started? With three fascinating characteristics of laser beams; stimulated emission (excite and energize), coherency (tune dialogue), and collimation (zoom in). These qualities work together to create a laser beam that is long and strong. Focused to the max and accurate enough to remove diseased tissue from a human body without harming nearby healthy tissue. If the laser does not have all three properties, it won't work. Without energy, the photons would not be generated. Without coherency, the light would be a jumble of colors on differing wavelengths. And without collimation, the light would spread out and become diffuse.

If you want to focus like a laser beam, you need all three characteristics. Without energy, your team will not be able to engage in the work or be productive. Without tuned dialogue, conversation will not support creativity, problem solving, and success. And without zooming in, you and your team will be wasting your precious time doing work that does not make a difference.

These qualities of focus feed off one another, too. Great dialogue improves your ability to prioritize, and it energizes participants. Focusing on the most important tasks makes people feel better about their jobs and ensures that conversations are more relevant. Energy and engagement fuel great dialogue and task selection. The ten ways to do what matter most may seem unrelated, but they come together to form a synergistic, self-reinforcing, and powerful way to work. When you focus like a laser beam, you set yourself up to make a significant contribution to your business and your employees' work lives—and your own.

References

Books and Articles

Andreotti, L., and Hilgendorf, B. *Sex, Intimacy and Business*. Edmonds, Wash.: Brilliance Press, 2006.

Bell, C. "The Vulnerable Leader." *Leader to Leader*, 2005, 38, 19–23.

Carnegie, D. *How to Win Friends and Influence People* (rev. ed.). New York: Pocket Books, 1990.

Csele, M. *Fundamentals of Light Sources and Lasers*. Hoboken, N.J.: Wiley, 2004.

Csikszentmihalyi, M. *Good Business*. New York: Penguin, 2004.

Drucker, P. *The Effective Executive*. New York: HarperCollins, 2002.

Farson, R. *Management of the Absurd*. New York: Simon & Schuster, 1996.

Ferrazzi, K. *Never Eat Alone*. New York: Currency Doubleday, 2005.

Frankl, V. *Man's Search for Meaning*. New York: Pocket Books, 1997. (Originally published 1946.)

Goldratt, E. *Critical Chain*. Great Barrington, Mass.: North River Press, 1997.

Hemsath, D., and Yerkes, L. *301 Ways to Have Fun at Work*. San Francisco: Berrett-Koehler, 1997.

Kabat-Zinn, J. *Coming to Our Senses*. New York: Hyperion, 2005.

Kopeikina, L. *The Right Decision Every Time*. Upper Saddle River, N.J.: Prentice Hall, 2005.

Lerner, H. *The Dance of Intimacy*. New York: Harper Paperbacks, 1990.

Lewis, D. *Free Your Breath, Free Your Life*. Boston: Shambala, 2004.

Lewis, L. *The Trader Joe's Adventure*. Chicago: Dearborn Trade Books, 2005.

Liebertz, C. "Want Clear Thinking? Relax." *Scientific American Mind*, 2005, 11, 88–89.

Madson, P. *Improv Wisdom*. New York: Crown, 2005.

McFarland, J. "Is Multitasking Overrated?" *Harvard Management Update*, June 1, 2002.

Moore, J. "Simple Ideas, Lightly Held." In T. Sattersten, *More Space: Nine Antidotes to Complacency in Business*. Mukwonago, Wisc.: Astronaut Projects, 2005.

Perkins, D. *Archimedes' Bathtub*. New York: Norton, 2000.

Rubinstein, J. S., Meyer, D. E., and Evans, J. E. "Executive Control of Cognitive Processes in Task Switching," *Journal of Experimental Psychology: Human Perception and Performance,* 2001, *27*(4), 763–787. Available online: http://www.apa.org/journals/releases/xhp274763.pdf. Access date: Feb. 14, 2006.

Sanders, T. *The Likeability Factor.* New York: Crown, 2005.

Santosus, M. "Why More Is Less." *CIO Magazine,* Sept. 2003, p. 15.

Sattersten, T. *More Space.* Milwaukee, Wisc.: Astronaut Projects, 2005.

Zeer, D. *Office Yoga.* San Francisco: Chronicle Books, 2000.

Weblogs and Web sites

Blohowiak, D. "Beyond Staff Meetings." *Leadership Now.* October 27, 2005. Available online: http://blogs.bnet.com/leadershipnow/?m=200510. Access date: January 13, 2006.

Copp, C., Agpaoa, C., Carvalho, S., and Pfeiffer, W. "Staff Empowerment, A Prescription for Success." *Permanente Journal.* Fall 2003. Available online: http://xnet.kp.org/permanentejournal/. Access date: January 13, 2006.

Goldsmith, M. "Feed Forward." *Leadership Excellence,* 2003. Available online: http://www.marshallgoldsmithlibrary.com/. Access date: January 13, 2006.

Goldsmith, M. "Let it Go." *Leadership Excellence,* 2005. Available online: http://www.marshallgoldsmithlibrary.com/. Access date: January 13, 2006.

Haneberg, L. "Managing Outside the Box." Management Craft, September 29, 2005. Available online: http://managementcraft.typepad.com/management_craft/. Access date: January 13, 2006.

Rodriguez, E. "Focus Schmocus." *Crossroads Dispatches.* October 24, 2005. Available online: http://evelynrodriguez.typepad.com/. Access date: January 13, 2006.

Row, H. "Squidoo Beta: Wave One." Squidblog. October 17, 2005. Available online: http://www.squidoo.com/blog/. Access date: January 13, 2006.

Savage, A. "Coyote Tries Multitasking." *The Coyote Within.* October 26, 2005. Available online: http://www.adriansavage.com/blog. Access date: January 13, 2006.

The Author

Lisa Haneberg is an expert in the areas of management, leadership, and personal and organizational success. In addition to consulting on organization development, management and leadership training, and human resources, she offers integrated training solutions and individual and group coaching services and speaks on a variety of leadership and management topics.

Her first book, *High Impact Middle Management: Solutions for Today's Busy Managers*, was a groundbreaking management book for its audience (Adams Media, January 2005). She has also written *Organization Development Basics* (September 2005) and *Coaching Basics* (March 2006) for the ASTD Press. She was one of eleven contributors to *More Space* (October 2005), a book of essays written by some of the brightest minds in business. Haneberg reaches a worldwide audience through her blog, Management Craft (www.managementcraft.com and www.allbusiness.com). Management Craft offers resources and perspectives to leaders, managers, and those who develop and coach them. Her main Web site, www.lisahaneberg.com, highlights her products and services.

Over the past twenty-two years, Haneberg has worked with leaders at all levels and for many types and sizes of organizations including high-tech manufacturing (Intel); distribution, manufacturing, and services (Black & Decker, Mead Paper); e-retailing and distribution (Amazon.com); travel and leisure products and services (Beacon Hotel, Travcoa, and Cruise West); and the Royal Government of Thailand. She is a certified master trainer and behavioral assessment interpreter. She earned an undergraduate degree in behavioral sciences from the University of Maryland and has taken graduate courses at Johns Hopkins University and Ohio State University.

She lives in the beautiful Pacific Northwest with her husband, four dogs, and two cats. She enjoys travel, reading, writing, and driving her convertible down winding roads.

Index